Frank Barrett

Lieutenant Barnabas

Vol. III

Frank Barrett

Lieutenant Barnabas
Vol. III

ISBN/EAN: 9783337040192

Printed in Europe, USA, Canada, Australia, Japan

Cover: Foto ©ninafisch / pixelio.de

More available books at **www.hansebooks.com**

LIEUTENANT BARNABAS.

A NOVEL.

BY

FRANK BARRETT.

AUTHOR OF "FOLLY MORRISON," ETC.

IN THREE VOLUMES.
VOL. III.

LONDON:
RICHARD BENTLEY AND SON,
NEW BURLINGTON STREET.
1881.
Right of Translation Reserved.

CONTENTS

OF

THE THIRD VOLUME.

CHAPTER	PAGE
I.—Ill Tidings	1
II.—Dr. Blandly in Stanhope Street	21
III.—Lady Betty reaches a Turning Point	30
IV.—A Friend in Need.	54
V.—Gerard Talbot	68
VI.—The Taming of Mrs. Baxter	93
VII.—Lady Betty's Visit	109
VIII.—Brother and Sister	129
IX.—In Tom's Place	143
X.—Barnabas and his Court	159
XI.—The Meeting of Old Friends.	175
XII.—Flight and Pursuit	194
XIII.—Quick and Dead	209
XIV.—Pandora's Box	222
XV.—Gerard Turns his Face to the Wall	233
XVI.—The Omen	245
XVII.—A Sturdy Rogue	259
XVIII.—Farewell	269
XIX.—In the Library	279
XX.—" Greater Love hath no Man than this, that a Man lay down his Life for his Friends"	290

LIEUTENANT BARNABAS.

CHAPTER I.

ILL TIDINGS.

MRS. WALKER stood in her drawing-room arranging the ribbons of her elegant bonnet before a glass. Lady Betty sat near a window working at a strip of embroidery.

"Once more, Lady Betty, will you accompany me?" asked Mrs. Walker.

"Once more, Felicia, and at the risk of being thought ungrateful, no."

"'Twill be the best and genteelest entertainment of the season."

"I hope you will enjoy it. You shall tell me all about it to-morrow; that will increase your pleasure."

"You can change your dress in half an hour, and I shall wait willingly."

"Why do you press me? 'Tis a waste of sweetness, like singing to the drowsy."

"It has been said that my singing would cure the drowsy of their weakness. If I thought my powers of persuasion were equally potent I would not tire until I had cured you."

"Why should you take such pains?"

"Because your symptoms are grave, and gravity of any sort is repugnant to me."

"Is there no season when it becomes one to be grave?"

"Yes; but happily the season does not

set in before forty." Mrs. Walker seated herself.

"You will be late, Felicia."

"No; the invitation was for four, and 'tis only on the stroke of six. I think I shall set the fashion of stating the hour at which an entertainment is to close instead of that at which it should commence. 'Twould be more reasonable."

"Then for your own sake do nothing of the sort; for if you are suspected of being reasonable you will certainly be convicted of being unfashionable."

"Ah me! Your case is very bad indeed," sighed Mrs. Walker. "How long do you think it will be, Lady Betty, before you smile again?"

"I cannot say; for the sake of appearances I hope I shall not smile again—before I find something to smile at."

"My dear, I know the secret of your gravity and sarcasm, and shall take upon myself to give you a lecture. You are thinking about that ill-mannered young gentleman, Mr. Tom Talbot."

"I do not know any ill-mannered gentleman of that name."

"Well, we will not call him a gentleman, if the definition is incorrect—this highly-respectable barbarian who was called to order by our friend Gerard Crewe for insulting you."

"Who told you that?" asked Lady Betty, quickly.

"No one. I drew my conclusion, which seems to be correct, from the fact that neither you nor Mr. Crewe would give me any information of what occurred in the library when the challenge was given. Our barbarian does not conceal his faults, and we can imagine how he would misbehave himself if his untamed passions were provoked. The offence was so unpardonable that Mr. Crewe found it necessary to punish him. At that moment you had every reason to be satisfied. Your affront was about to be avenged; a well-bred gentleman undertook to risk his life as your champion, and make you the talk of society, and the envy of your friends. But with strange perversity you closed your eyes to the advantages of your position, and lost your senses as completely as Ophelia. To be sure you didn't drown yourself; but that was no fault of yours, you got as wet as you could. When the result of the meeting was known, your joy was almost as terrible as your fears had been. Altogether, for about twenty-four hours you suffered as much romantic emotion as the heroine of a tragedy—and for whom? For the gentleman who risked his life for your honour—who spared his rival for your sake—who waits upon you day by day with untiring devotion—whose generous love, unencouraged by a single smile, unrewarded by one word of acknowledgement, seeks constantly to gratify your unexpressed desires—who bears with you patiently in your womanly follies and caprice, and takes your passive tolerance as the guerdon of his affection—a gentleman, handsome, well-bred, and gracious —was it in his peril you suffered—in his safety you rejoiced? No. 'Twas for a man the very opposite of him—a man rough and rude as the savage from the woods, intolerant and unappreciative, a tyrant who would be a slave, a slave who would be a tyrant; a barbarian, who having offended does not seek forgiveness, who having frightened you to desperation, values your sympathy so little that he leaves you in despair and allows his rival to relieve your fears ——"

" You exaggerate to extravagance."

"I deny it. Who was it came to tranquilise your mind after the meeting—the man you loved or the man that loved you?"

"Gerard does not love me in the sense that you imply. He is my friend simply."

"And mine also; but if he paid me the same attention my husband would not be jealous without a cause. What extravagance can you prove against me? Is it not the bare truth that from the day he affronted you, Mr. Talbot has not once called upon you?"

"I forbade—that is—it was my wish that he should cease to visit me."

"I do not take obedience as a proof of love, nor you either. Tell me candidly why you have refused invitations since the meeting; why you have stayed within doors from morning until night; why you start when you hear a visitor arrive; and, lastly, tell me why you are sitting by that open window? You are silent—your conscience tells you that you expect him to disobey."

"My conscience tells me nothing of the sort. You are quite wrong, Felicia."

"Then why do you refuse to accompany me this afternoon? Be candid, Lady Betty—you owe me an explanation. You will find me more indulgent as a confidant than as a successful inquisitor, and I assure you I never suffer my curiosity to rest unsatisfied."

"'Tis not fear of ridicule that makes me reticent," said Lady Betty, after a few moments of thoughtful silence. "But on some subjects we differ so completely that it is useless to discuss them—and painful also when one feels deeply. However, I will not suffer my reserve to reduce you to the unamiable task of examining into the secrets of your friend."

"Thank you, my dear," Mrs. Walker replied, with a graceful bow.

"I do love Mr. Talbot. I love him with all my heart. You would like to know why. It is a question I have hardly asked myself. I admire him for those very barbaric qualities that you deprecate, perhaps for qualities that you have not recognised, and would not admire if you did."

"I should like to know them all the same."

"Strength of heart, fidelity, trust ——"

"Et cetera. He has no fault, I suppose?"

"None that time will not remove."

"Well, thank the stars you may outlive him by a dozen years. Go on, dear."

"There is no act of his that I cannot justify ——"

"Even to his late neglect?"

"'Tis not neglect, but the faithful execution of a plan which we conceived necessary to my happiness. I acknowledge that after the duel I hoped he would break through his resolution and come to me; now I rejoice that he was stronger than me."

"I see. It is the fear that he may yet succumb which makes you so anxious when a knock at the door announces a visitor; and you refuse to leave the house in order that you may not lose the opportunity of reprimanding him for his error if he should come, hey?"

"No. I do not expect him, nor hope ——" She stopped abruptly as the sound of a voice upon the stairs reached her ears.

Mrs. Walker laughed lightly and kept her eyes fixed on Lady Betty's anxious face. The door opened, and the servant announced:

"Mr. Gerard Crewe."

A ray of satisfaction lit up Lady Betty's face, much to the perplexity of Mrs. Walker.

Gerard entered, went through the form of salutation mechanically, and took a seat in silence. Lady Betty felt that she was being watched, and took up the embroidery in her trembling fingers. Unusually constrained and ill at ease, Gerard fixed his eyes on her for a moment, dropped them, raised them again, without opening his lips. Highly amused with a fancied discovery, Mrs. Walker after contemplating the two friends for some moments, rose, saying with a malicious smile:

"Mr. Crewe, you will forgive me, I am sure, if I leave you to the entertainment of Lady Betty." Then crossing to Lady Betty, she said a few words of farewell, and bending down to kiss her, added in a whisper:

"I understand now why you do not wish Mr. Talbot to return. You are a more consummate coquette than I thought. May the best man win, dear."

Gerard closed the door after Mrs. Walker, and took a seat near Lady Betty, saying:

"My mission has taken me longer than I expected, and I have only painful news to give you."

"Painful news?" murmured Lady Betty, as if uncertain of what she heard.

"You must summon your fortitude to hear that which my tongue must falter to tell."

"Tom is ill!" She rose quickly and threw aside her work, as though prepared to go at once to the relief of the man she loved."

"It is not illness. Sit down, Lady Betty, unfortunately you can do nothing to lessen the calamity."

"That word is ill-chosen, if he is not ill. Tell me what has happened without hesitation. I am prepared for painful news. You have not found Tom, or he has left England—but that is not a calamity and I can hear worse than that bravely."

"A misfortune that leaves us hope is to be borne ——"

Lady Betty interrupted him; laying her hand upon his arm, and speaking scarcely above her breath, she asked:

"Is Tom dead?"

"We can only hope that is he not."

"Ah, you are trying to break the fall of this blow. You are concealing the truth from me. I know all; I read it in your trembling lips and pitying eye—Tom is dead. My poor fond Tom is lost to me for ever. Be merciful and tell me the truth with cruel words that my heart may break with the shock."

"Be calm—there is hope."

"Oh, God bless you for that word, you good friend—dear Gerard! What a foolish girl am I to think the worst at a mere word; scold me, Gerard, for my folly."

"My poor child—there is hope, but it is so slight ——"

"That it were better there was none! True. Why should we encourage a fearful suspense. Let us realise the truth at once and not believe the fact. Tom is dead, is he not?"

"It may be best to think so, indeed."

Lady Betty fixed her eyes upon Gerard in a bewilderment of agony, and was silent for a moment, then taking his hand between hers she said in low reproach:

"Oh Gerard—we loved each other, we two—Tom with his whole heart, and I with mine, and love is more than life. For two to die is nothing, but for me to live and lose, is terrible. Think, I lost my mother but two months since, would you add to that loss a greater still? Tell me, he is not dead—cheat my senses for a little while with seeming truths. I am simple and easily beguiled. You shake your head, and yet you profess to love me. Can you see me suffer, and offer no word of consolation—I do not weep, but I suffer here—here at my heart, beating slow and leaden as though the life had gone out with the love he planted there. Pity me! give me a word of comfort, for I cannot cry. You have tears in your eyes, and suffer too but not as I do. Say a word to me, no matter what—but do not look at me in silent sorrow, so."

"I will tell you all that has happened, and you shall use your woman's wit to catch the rays of hope."

"Yes, yes—I will listen calmly and patiently—tell me all, leave not a word unsaid. Hide nothing, be the facts ever so ghastly. Women are strong in scenes of terror, and do not shudder to look upon a gaping wound that they may find the means to heal."

"I will tell you faithfully all that has occurred since I left you on Tuesday. I knew that if anyone could tell me where to find our friend Tom it would be Dr. Blandly, and I went first to Edmonton where he lives. There I learnt that the Doctor had left home hastily and gone to Talbot Hall in Kent, on business of urgent importance. I followed him and arrived at Talbot Hall the same night. Doctor Blandly was in deep distress, for Tom who has been staying at the Hall since we last saw him, was missing, and up to that moment no trace of him found. On Wednesday afternoon, he left the Hall to dine with a friend at Maidstone. Late at night, as the steward's daughter was watching at her window, Tom's mare ran up riderless to the lodge gate. Her knees were cut, and her saddle wet. The steward started off at once to make inquiries at Maidstone, and found that Tom had left his friend about ten o'clock. As soon as it was light a search was begun. The steward took the first London coach and sought Doctor Blandly. When he arrived, a few hours before me, nothing had been discovered. While he was telling me this, the steward returned to the Hall bringing with him Tom's hat, which had been found in a sluice some distance below Maidstone. It was conjectured then that he had followed the upper bank of the river, and in attempting to ford it had been carried away by the force of the current."

"But he could swim. He was master of all manly exercises. Oh! I know he is safe! Why do you despair?—for you do: your face tells me so."

"Yesterday morning as soon as it was light, the search was recommenced. The keeper of the bridge-gate believed that a gentleman on horse had crossed the bridge at ten, and while some explored the path below the bridge, where poor Tom's hat had been found, others examined the tow-path which leads on the lower side of the river towards a bye-road communicating with the neighbourhood of Talbot Hall. It was there that we found new traces. There was a broken cord upon the posts of an old gateway. On the river bank beside it were the marks of a horse's hoofs, and a little further on the reeds were crushed and broken, foot-prints were upon the bank, and a trail by the rushes as though a heavy body had been drawn over the soft mud."

"That showed that he had drawn himself from the water."

"I fear not—the herbage and rushes

were depressed and matted in the yielding clay towards the water, and not from it."

"Then what do you conclude?"

"A week or ten days since Tom was shot at in a wood; and it is only too greatly to be feared that the same murderous hand stretched the cord across the path which threw Tom's mare, and afterwards dragged his lifeless body into the river."

"Oh, Heavens! What else have you to tell?"

"Nothing. We found no more."

"You only confirm my despair. You leave me no space for hope."

"One fact alone forbids despair; we have not found Tom's body. The river has been dragged between the place where he was thrown, and the sluice where his hat was discovered, without result. It is possible that he was only stunned by the fall from his mare, and restored to consciousness by the immersion in the river he saved himself by swimming to the bank."

"Why that is more than possible—it must be so."

"But he has not returned to the Hall. And we have inquired at the inns beside the river for miles, and no one has seen him."

"Then all is lost."

"The current is strong, for the river has been swollen by the heavy rains of last week, and our one hope is, that when consciousness returned to him he was far down the river. Exhausted, perhaps hurt, he may be waiting in some remote cottage until he has sufficient strength to return to us."

"I pray God it may be so," said Lady Betty, clasping her hands, and speaking with all the fervour of her soul.

Gerard bent his head, and added his silent prayer to hers.

CHAPTER II.

DOCTOR BLANDLY IN STANHOPE STREET.

FORTNIGHT later Doctor Blandly called at the house in Stanhope Street, presented his card, and asked to see Miss Elizabeth St. Cyr. He was shown into the reception-room. The Doctor advanced to the middle of the room, and standing there looked round him with the curiosity of a student who has learnt to gauge the character of people by the things they use in their every-day life.

"Very elegant, very elegant indeed,"

said he, running his eye over the furniture and appointments, "and about as hideous as the mind of man can conceive."

He took off his glasses to rub them before examining the pictures more closely, and was still polishing them with his yellow silk handkerchief when the door opened, and Mrs. Walker entered the room.

"Doctor Blandly, I presume," she said, with an amiable smile.

The Doctor adjusted his glasses carefully upon his nose, looked at Mrs. Walker attentively, and then answered:

"Yes, that is my name; but unless I am greatly mistaken in your age, you are not the young woman I have come to see."

Unaccustomed to plain speaking, Mrs. Walker for a moment could not decide whether to resent or pass over Doctor

Blandly's brusquerie; however, her curiosity to know the object of his visit induced her to regard him merely as an amusing original.

"I am Mrs. Walker, the bosom friend of Lady Betty, who is now, at my persuasion, taking the air, but I expect her to return shortly."

"In that case I will wait for Miss St. Cyr, if you will allow me."

Mrs. Walker made a courteous reply, and begged her visitor to take a chair. The Doctor scanned the collection of chairs, and selecting one from the further end of the room which seemed more trustworthy to sit upon than the rest, he placed it in front of Mrs. Walker and seated himself, saying:

"If the frames of your chairs were as stout as the frames of your pictures, madam, there would be less danger in using them for their legitimate purpose;

if this room were mine, I would make a bench of the pictures, and hang up the chairs to look at."

"You object to elegance, Doctor Blandly."

"No, madam; for elegance, as I take it, is that perfect harmony of one part with another which we find in Nature's handiwork; but where is the harmony between my figure and the chair I sit upon with trembling? 'Tis as if one set the legs of a gazelle under the body of an elephant."

"You are a humourist, Doctor Blandly."

The Doctor made a stiff bow, took a pinch of snuff, and showed no inclination to re-open the conversation. Mrs. Walker felt that she must either leave him or come to direct questions.

"May I ask if you have made any discovery relative to poor Mr. Talbot?" she asked.

"None. We have found not a sign nor trace since the second day of our search."

Doctor Blandly heaved a sigh, looked on the ground with raised eyebrows, and tapped the table with his fingers, while Mrs. Walker asked herself what could be the object of his visit to Lady Betty.

"I am naturally very deeply interested in the unfortunate gentleman, for Lady Betty was deeply attached to him, and is inconsolable for his loss."

"Inconsolable, madam? and he has been lost a fortnight!" exclaimed Doctor Blandly, with awakened interest.

"I assure you 'tis true. I have done all I could to make her forget him, but in vain. She refuses to go to the opera, to Ranelagh, to tea-parties, to routs, and secludes herself in her own room when I have visitors."

"I can scarcely understand a friend of yours being dull to such attractions."

"Yet 'tis the fact," said Mrs. Walker, acknowledging the compliment with a bow. "I admit that my patience is almost exhausted."

"Such obstinacy would try the patience of a saint."

"And 'tis entirely for her own sake that I use my persuasions. She is wasting her time, perhaps jeopardizing her future happiness, by giving way to these morbid regrets, which avail nothing. Tears cannot revive the dead."

"The truest words you ever spoke, madam."

"I am glad to find that you agree with me, Doctor Blandly."

"I hope you will never find me wanting in sense, Mrs. Walker."

Mrs. Walker flirted her fan, and greatly encouraged by the Doctor's ambiguity, which she interpreted as a compliment to herself, proceeded :

"Lady Betty is in a position to make an admirable match. She is young, pretty, and has, it seems, a very useful little fortune. She might reasonably hope to marry a young man of title : that was, I believe, her mother's dying wish, and the dying wish of a mother should be observed as a sacred duty, in my opinion ; what do you think, Doctor ?"

Doctor Blandly considered the sanctity of a mother's dying wish unquestionable.

"Now Mr. Talbot, although possessed of a good estate, had no title, and his behaviour in company was most awkward. He could not conform himself with the habits of society, and when he tried to do so he made himself ridiculous. He had a habit of contradicting people, and setting them right if they happened to make errors, which was extremely provoking, and he absolutely went to sleep in his seat during a very elegant performance of an oratorio by amateurs of distinguished rank. He made no secret of his dislike to the modern usages of London society, and I have not the slightest doubt that had he married Lady Betty he would have taken her away for nine months out of the twelve, to spend one half her time in a country Hall where it was impossible to keep awake, and the other half in foreign cities, where it was impossible to go to sleep. And so, to be quite candid, I must admit that—for her sake—I am not sorry to hear that you have not found Mr. Talbot. This morbid condition is not natural to her, and if we are fortunate enough to hear no more of Mr. Talbot, she will soon recover her health and spirits, and we may hope to find her a suitable husband amongst the many admirers she is sure to find at the Wells, where I propose to take her next month. You don't think it probable that Mr. Talbot is alive, Doctor Blandly?"

"I cannot hope!"

"Nor I, neither. Nothing is further from my hopes, I assure you, and so let us trust that we have heard the last of him, and that he is in a happier world."

"You may rely upon your devout wish being gratified. If, as you hope, Mr. Talbot is in a better world than this, rest assured, madam, that you have seen the last of him."

CHAPTER III.

LADY BETTY REACHES A TURNING-POINT.

HEN Lady Betty returned from her drive, she was met in the hall by Mrs. Walker.

"My dear Lady Betty, a gentleman is waiting to see you."

Lady Betty's heart leaped and her lip trembled. She had not yet relinquished the hope that Tom would return to her.

"A gentleman!" she echoed.

"An old gentleman. A perfect original. A most amusing old quiz, I protest. Doctor Blandly."

"Has he brought me news?"

"Not a word. I have been trying for the last half-hour to discover the object of his visit, but either he is very stupid or very ill-mannered, for I could get nothing out of him. I am inclined to think from his concluding observations that he considers himself clever. He is in the reception-room; go, my dear, and see what you can make of him."

Lady Betty opened the door at once, and found herself for the first time face to face with Doctor Blandly. Her mother's description of him as he appeared in his gardening dress had led her to imagine him an untidy, coarse old man; it astonished her to find him as he was—a particularly neat, fair-complexioned, portly gentleman, with a shapely leg, a handsome satin waistcoat, a snowy frill, and a well-curled wig.

She made him a low courtesy, which he

acknowledged, and then drawing near the window, he placed a chair for her in the light, where he could see her more perfectly. She took the seat, and he, bringing his chair directly in front of her, seated himself, and after looking at her pale, anxious face for a moment in silence, said:

"Your face tells me who you are, young lady, not from its resemblance to any face that I have seen, but that it answers to my expectations, and, let me add, my hopes. You are the Lady Betty that poor Tom gave his heart to."

Lady Betty's chin twitched; she tried to answer, failed, and dropped her head upon her bosom as the tears started to her eyes.

"Do not speak; I will do all the talking for awhile. I am Doctor Blandly. Give me your hand, so. Let us who were strangers to each other be friends. Tom has left a space in our hearts that we must seek to fill with new affections. He was dear to me, and I am an old man, but to you, with younger thoughts and sympathies ——"

"He was my life. I did not know how dear he was to me. I am like a child learning to value blessings by their loss."

"'Tis an unfinished lesson to the oldest," said Doctor Blandly, gently. The tone of commiseration touched her to the heart. His sympathy was the first she had received. Gerard had sought only to console her; Mrs. Walker endeavoured to reason her out of suffering; other friends she had none. She cried freely now, and Doctor Blandly did not attempt to restrain her tears. Purposely the old pathologist lanced her wound, knowing the relief it would produce, and he encouraged the outflow of her grief by gentle words of pity. After awhile her weeping ended in a long, shuddering sigh, and she wiped her eyes with a brave resolve to cry no more. But her soul was full of gratitude to the pitying Doctor; she pressed his hands between her moist, hot palms, and looking in his face wondered how any one could mistake him for a misanthrope and a woman-hater.

"No man who disliked women could be so womanly tender," she thought; "no wonder Tom loved him." Then her thoughts returned to her lost lover. "You have brought me no hopeful news?" she asked, wistfully.

"No, my child; the news I have to give you is not good."

"Has his body been found?"

"Even that poor consolation is denied us. It is concluded that he was carried by the current far down the river, and that the shore-folk robbed him of his clothes, and sunk his corpse to avoid inquiry. We shall never know where he lies."

Lady Betty, sighing, shook her head and lapsed into a reverie, which Doctor Blandly did not interrupt. He wished her to exhaust her present grief before opening the subject which had brought him to her.

"No mound of green turf to mark his resting-place, no spot where one might cherish flowers to his memory," murmured she.

"He has your tears. A marble is not needed to keep his memory sacred in your heart."

"I do not know, Doctor Blandly, I am not sure of myself. I wished to die when I heard that he was dead, but I live. This morning, though I did not eat, I felt quite hungry. Perhaps I shall cease to grieve one day."

"I hope so; you are too young and too healthy to brood long upon your sorrow."

"But 'tis heartless to forgot the one we love."

"'Tis evil to repine when nature bids us smile. Be true to yourself, child; weep when you grieve, eat when you are hungry, laugh when you are pleased. Leave false sentiment to false people—to creatures who cumber the earth and do no good in it; to fools who cramp their souls, as the Chinese cramp their feet for fashion's sake; fools like the woman of this house here, who could put on a pious enthusiasm and lay aside her Godless indifference if the mode changed."

The Doctor frowned, took out his snuff-box, and tapped it angrily. Lady Betty opened her eyes in astonishment at the rapid transition of his temper.

"Come, I don't wish to frighten you,"

he said, in a subdued tone, catching the startled expression on her face. "You have a rough old doctor to deal with, who has seen such grievous miseries in the world that he has lost pity for sham ailments, and those who will not be well. Your body is weak, probably by fasting when you should have been eating, and that accounts for the gloomy hopes of perpetual sorrow that you wish to encourage. Eat and drink, my dear, and sleep when you may. Be strong and brave to the utmost of your power, and, above all, be true to nature and yourself. The angels shall acquit you of heartlessness, and your own conscience will be satisfied."

Then the Doctor took his pinch of snuff, replaced the box quietly in his pocket, and dusted himself carefully with his India handkerchief. Lady Betty watched the play of his features with furtive glances, until he fixed his eyes on her face, and looked at her with troubled uncertainty.

"My dear," said he—"I have news for you, concerning your temporal position, which will give you trouble; and I am in hesitation whether to tell you now or to wait until your health is more robust."

"I can bear to hear anything now, Doctor Blandly."

"Well, then, you shall hear what your friend Mrs. Walker has been endeavouring to find out for half an hour and more. In the first, I presume that you know nothing of the pecuniary position in which you were placed at your mother's death."

"She told me that she had placed her property in your hands for disposal, and her attorney sent me a sum of money about a month since, as a quarterly payment of the interest arising from it.

That is all I know. After mamma's death I was too troubled for a time to think of such trifles, and he—Tom assured me one day that I need not bestow any thought upon the matter."

"If he were living it would still be unnecessary. Your mamma loved you very much, my child, but she was not a wise woman, nor a considerate woman. It was her dream that she should see you married to a wealthy husband before she died. To realise that dream she considered it necessary to occupy a position in society which the mere per-centage of her money could not procure."

"Doctor Blandly—are you obliged to tell me this?"

"I do not willingly undertake a painful task; it is only because I think it necessary that I disclose the fact which others besides your mother have tried to keep secret. You cannot accept, without inquiry a bare statement of the consequences attending your mother's inconsiderate act?"

"Tell me the result, and let me question afterwards if it is necessary."

"When the money you have now is spent, you will be penniless.

"Penniless," echoed Lady Betty, unable at once to grasp the meaning of the word.

"You have nothing more to receive. Do you comprehend all which that implies?"

"I will try to do so—when my purse is empty I shall have nothing to give the servant who waits on me; when my dresses are worn out—if I wish to leave my friend—if I stay—oh!" she clasped her hands as she realised that henceforth she must depend upon hospitality for a roof and charity for clothes.

"Shall I explain how this comes about?" asked the Doctor coldly.

"No," she cried with quickened energy. "If my degradation is due to any act of my mother's let it be hid for ever."

"Remember the money was entrusted to me—a perfect stranger to your mother."

"But not to Tom nor—nor to me. I am content to accept the result of my mother's act without questioning her love or your honour."

Doctor Blandly bowed, but his forehead lost none of its creases, and he resorted to his snuff-box for the means of solving the difficulty before him.

"I am afraid," said he, "that you will not get that inquisitive woman, Mrs. Walker, to accept the result with your magnanimity, Miss Betty."

"It is no business of hers."

"That is precisely my reason for expecting her to meddle with it to a very considerable extent. If you know how to cope with all the subtle attacks of an idle, curious, unprincipled woman, I am content to leave the matter as it stands."

"If I tell her that I have lost my fortune, and refuse to explain how, what can she learn?"

"The truth possibly. If not she will imagine a cause, and publish it as a fact to sustain her own reputation. Does she know that I acted for your mother?"

"Yes—she asked me, and I told her."

Doctor Blandly smiled, and rising from his chair said—"Well well, we will see what happens. If in a week a lie circulates and reaches your ear, I shall be happy to disprove it."

"Wait—I see what might happen. It did not strike me at first. You might be accused of misappropriating the money."

"Oh, I should take no notice of that," replied the Doctor, sturdily. "That's a lie that could do you no harm. What I fear is, that the woman may resent your silence, and lay the blame upon you, or—one who is dearer to you perhaps, than yourself."

"You mean Tom. But how could she introduce his name into an affair with which he had nothing to do?"

"She might discover that he had something to do with it?"

"A word from you would disprove that."

"You are in error—I could not disprove it by any number of words."

"You shall tell me all. How can he be concerned."

"You wish me now to tell you all."

"Yes—I—I—I am not consistent perhaps, but I could not rest with anything that concerns *him* untold."

"There is little to shock you in what I have to tell—and take this from me, my dear Miss Betty—concealment is more terrible than revelation; no harm ever was done by telling and knowing the truth, but from blinking it there has been more misery on this earth than you can suppose. When we admit that your mother was loving and unwise, we give her blame and praise, that reduces her no lower than the level of womankind. To be deeply loving and deeply wise at the same time, seems hardly possible to our humanity. Look at your mother as a woman whose love exceeded her wisdom, and you can hardly regret her folly."

A faint smile of gratitude passed over Lady Betty's face, and she nodded her head.

"Your mother, influenced by her hopes for your welfare, against my dissuasions determined on investing all her money in an annuity terminable at her death. She would not believe that her tenure of life was uncertain, though I warned her of her danger, and allowed my temper to express itself in no measured terms.

"Seeing the ruin that impended over you, I resolved to purchase the annuity with a sum of money Tom Talbot had desired me to invest for him, knowing that he would be just, and more than that, generous towards you. He knew nothing of the contract until your mother's death. I wished him to refund what remained of your mother's capital; but to spare you the knowledge of your mother's indiscretion he refused the proposition, and desired that the annuity should be extended to you."

"Oh! my good, generous Tom."

"Alas, you have reason now to regret his generosity. Had he followed my advice you would now have had sufficient to secure you a moderate income."

"Then I thank God I have nothing!"

"Hum! You have not learnt much from the teaching of Mrs. Walker, or it has been of a negative kind. I doubt if any amount of generous sentiments would compensate her for the loss of eighteen-pence."

"He could have obliged me to sever myself from the society he disliked had he chosen to exercise the power he possessed."

"He might, Heaven be praised, Tom's faults were of a manly kind," said Doctor Blandly, sententiously. "Well, to come to the end of the poor fellow's praises, the day before his duel, he made me witness his will, which disposed of his property in two equal portions—one half for you, the other as I expect for me. Now don't cry again, my child—it was a foolish will, and

what the deuce he did with it no one
knows. In his modesty he omitted to
put my name in the document he showed
me, and after it was fairly set out he took
it away to insert the name. Possibly, he
destroyed it when he left the field safe and
sound; possibly he had it in one of his
pockets when he was thrown into the river,
the result is the same. No will is to be
found, and the whole estate reverts to his
next of kin. That next of kin has made
his appearance, and put in his claim.

"I am sorry to say his title cannot be
disputed. From him one can expect
neither generosity nor justice. He has a
sharp lawyer at his back, and every penny
to which the law entitles him will be
called in. And now, my child, you know
all my bad news."

Lady Betty smiled with a sigh of relief
to find the bad news so good. There was
nothing in it she regretted now. Even her

mother's fault seemed kind in the light thrown upon it by Doctor Blandly.

" You will wonder, Miss Betty," said Doctor Blandly, after a pause, in which he watched the young pale face attentively, " why I don't take my hat and bid you good morning. When a raven has croaked, the next thing expected of him is that he shall fly away. As I stay, you may take it that I have a better disposition than a raven. Will you tell me if you have any friends other than the woman of this house."

" Mr. Gerard Crewe is the only intimate friend."

" A young woman can scarcely open her mind to a young man, or ask services of him, and a young man whose gallantry would lead him to do your bidding whether it be good or bad, and whose breeding would silence his tongue when it was necessary to give you unpleasant advice, is not the friend you need. Try me, young lady, and don't be afraid of trying me a good deal." He held out his hand, and Lady Betty willingly gave him hers—feeling as he held it the significance of his grasp. " Now tell me the state of your affairs, and we will try and come to an arrangement for the future. How much money have you?"

" All that was sent to me by the gentleman in Lincoln's Inn."

" And how much do you owe?"

" I do not know—since mamma's death I have had dresses and bonnets, but Mrs. Walker said the tradesfolks could wait for their money."

" I warrant she did. Well, my dear, and did your mother leave any bills unpaid?"

" Yes, a great many."

" Did she now." The Doctor appeared to be greatly surprised. " But I daresay she gave a bill as well as received one. Do you think it possible that she gave a bill of sale upon her furniture and effects?"

"I received a letter yesterday concerning something of the kind, but I could not understand it. We didn't learn these matters in our arithmetic at school."

"No, my dear—knowledge of this kind does not come under the head of elegant accomplishments. But it should. Have you the letter?"

"It is in this pocket, I think. Yes—here."

Doctor Blandly read it through every word carefully, and folding it, said:

"This polite note informs you that Mr. M. Moss will be under the painful obligation of taking possession of all your house in Park Lane contains, unless the sum of three hundred pounds is paid by the 25th instant."

"Three hundred pounds! I have not so much."

"No, Miss Betty—no," the Doctor said, putting the letter in his pocket. "I will call upon Mr. M. Moss this afternoon, and see what can be done with him."

"Perhaps he will wait like the other tradesmen."

"I take it that Mr. M. Moss is a Jew; if he is, one cannot rank him with the other tradesmen, for Jews are scrupulously exact in collecting their debts and taking advantage of their opportunities."

"And my other debts!" Lady Betty was aghast as her eyes opened to the realities of her position.

"Collect all the bills you have, my dear, and let me have them. Not now, but when you are packing up your things to leave this house. By the way, will you do me the honour to be my visitor when you are free?"

Already the question, "Where am I to go?" had risen in Lady Betty's mind. This invitation came at the very moment it was needed.

"I shall be very glad to ——" She checked herself abruptly, struck by the sudden perception of her dependant position.

"Then that is settled," said the Doctor, briskly. "My house is too large for me. I will have two or three rooms prepared for you, and the sooner you come and take possession of them the better I shall like it."

"Doctor Blandly, I am very grateful for your kindness. I shall accept your advice and seek it without hesitation, and I shall be happy to visit you; but I beg you will not make any preparations, for my stay will be quite short."

Doctor Blandly was astonished by the altered tone in which she spoke—firm and self-reliant—and he looked at her curiously for a moment in silence; then he rose, and with a stiff bow answered :

" Very good, Miss Betty, very good," and taking a final pinch of snuff, he added to himself, " Proud as lucifer, for all her misfortunes."

Lady Betty seemed absorbed in thought, and so after a few minutes of unproductive conversation, Doctor Blandly left her, pressing her hand warmly when they parted, and reading the unspoken thoughts in her clear eyes. He was not displeased with what he read there.

It took Lady Betty longer to find out what had prompted her to refuse Doctor Blandly's hospitality, and to see that she had arrived at the turning point in her life.

CHAPTER IV.

A FRIEND IN NEED.

LADY BETTY ran with soft, quick steps past the drawing-room, and reached her room without interception, and sat there for half an hour after she had changed her riding-dress for an afternoon gown, with her hands in her lap and her eyes before her. Then she rose briskly and began to rummage her boxes and drawers where her papers were scattered—she was not a very orderly young person—selecting from among them the unpaid bills.

" Mistress is about to drink a dish of tea, and she wishes to know if you will join her as she is quite alone," said a servant at her door.

" Say I will be downstairs almost immediately," replied Lady Betty.

She waited but to close the open drawers and boxes, and then ran down to the drawing-room, folding the collected bills, and putting them away in her pocket.

" My dear Lady Betty, this cruel visit must have quite undone the good effects of your ride. I sympathise with you sincerely. Take this tea, my love, and tell me all about it. You found that dreadful old Doctor quite insupportable, I am sure," said Mrs. Walker.

" On the contrary, I found him very kind and considerate," replied Lady Betty, taking a seat at the table.

" I forgot that his interview was with

Lady Betty. It is quite impossible to be unamiable with you, my dear."

Lady Betty inclined her head, and showed no signs of being communicative.

" He came chiefly to offer you his sympathy, I suppose, dear?" said Mrs. Walker, returning undaunted to her charge.

" No, I think his main purpose was to speak about an affair of business. He was my poor mother's agent, as you know. By-the-bye, Felicia, you have some unpaid bills of mine, I think. Could you let me have them?"

" My love, they are in a hundred different places; it would take me a month to find them. You need not be anxious about them, they will be sent in again only too certainly."

" I would look for you, if you could tell me where to search."

" Why are you so eager to have them?"

"I wish to pay them."

"Then I shall certainly not let you have them. Don't look so preposterously grave, dear. The only pressing account is the dressmaker's, and we must pay that, or we shall never get our dresses home in time. There ought to be a law to bind dressmakers to punctuality, then we should not be put to this harassing necessity of paying bills whenever they are presented. She will be here tomorrow with the fashions to measure us for our travelling-dresses, and I will settle your bill at the same time with my own. Don't trouble yourself about the money, when we return from the Wells will suit me, or not at all, if you like it better."

"How good and generous all the world is!" thought Lady Betty, and involuntarily her tongue spoke her thought.

"What have you to be thankful for? —appreciation? That follows as the natural result of your mingling with people of taste. I object to gratitude, 'tis a mean, middle-class sentiment, an acknowledgement of inferiority which is unknown to us. We are equal; we are generous, and expect generosity; we accept services as our right. What style of bonnet shall you have for the journey?"

"I shall make my straw do."

"Straw! when nothing but beaver and silk is the rage? Nonsense! You shall not dress out of fashion just because you have a little trouble on your mind. I shall buy you a bonnet I saw this morning: 'tis a charming trifle, and with a mantle to match."

"Don't you think my tippet will answer all purposes, the weather is hot?"

"All the better reason for not dressing lightly. Never be *bourgeois* in your habits. But why should I tell you this, who have always shown such excellent taste and headed the fashions?"

"It is necessary for me to be economical."

"Oh, you are dreadfully, alarmingly shocking! Economical! what a horrid word!"

"Nevertheless, my circumstances oblige me to be saving."

"Another abominable expression, my dear. If at this moment you are pressed for money you must permit me to supply your wants. I have had property left to me, and I know what a long time it takes in passing through the lawyers' hands. I assure you that for six months after my father's demise I suffered unspeakable agonies, and I wished him back a hundred times, for I was at the mercy of his executors."

"I have enough money for my present necessities, thank you, Felicia."

"Then, in that case, you will have a silk bonnet, and whatever is the *bon ton* in dresses."

Lady Betty inclined her head in acquiescence. She had accepted to go to the Wells with Felicia, and she was bound to dress consistently.

Felicia bent forward and kissed her, pleased with her submission.

"When shall we leave London?" asked Lady Betty.

"In three weeks at the furthest, sooner, if our dresses are finished."

"And how long shall we stay there?"

"Until the end of the season. By that time you may reasonably hope to be in legal possession of your poor mother's property. I suppose Doctor Blandly is an executor?"

"No. My mother made no will. Poor soul! she had nothing to leave me."

"Nothing to leave you, Lady Betty! Why she was constantly talking about—"

" She made a very unfortunate speculation shortly before her death, which has resulted since in the loss of all she possessed."

" But she settled something upon you, surely ?"

" Not a penny, it was not in her power to do so."

" You have not whispered a word of this to me hitherto."

" I was ignorant myself until Doctor Blandly told me this afternoon."

" And you heard him without going into convulsions ? you did not even faint away ? and you can sit there and talk about it as calmly as if nothing had happened? Oh, I cannot believe it !"

" It is quite true."

" But you have some resource; Doctor

Blandly, perhaps, has promised you assistance?"

"I have no resource, in the sense you mean, and I cannot accept assistance from a gentleman unrelated to me by any ties of kindred or family friendship."

"That is an excellent reason for not offering assistance, but none for refusing it. One hears every day of persons making donations to perfect strangers, but I never yet heard of them being refused."

"I am not in a position to receive charity," said Lady Betty, rather sharply.

A proverb about beggars on horseback crossed Mrs. Walker's mind, but as she looked at her friend's young face and graceful figure, she was yet inclined to be hopeful, so she kept the reflection to herself, and said:

"'Tis a mercy you have good looks; with them and a little *finesse* you may manage to find a wealthy husband before the end of the season."

"Oh, Felicia! how can you for a moment think I could descend to such a baseness?"

"I see nothing base in marrying a wealthy husband." Mrs. Walker had married an old man for no better motive than the prospect of inheriting his riches. "It seems to me, Lady Betty, that poverty has exalted your sentiments to a prodigious extent, which is unfortunate, since, if there is one thing more than another that the poor cannot afford, and ought to get rid of, 'tis pride."

"On the contrary, I think 'tis the one thing they must retain to deserve respect."

Lady Betty spoke with warmth, and would probably have said much more, but that she was checked by the remembrance of Felicia's previous kindness, and a suspicion that she did not mean what she said.

"Then what on earth do you intend doing?"

"I have not yet had time to determine. Come, Felicia, be your natural self. We are alone, and worldliness is a mask that you put on to suit the cynical humour which is in fashion. Forget that you are Mrs. Walker, and advise me as Felicia."

"I have given my advice, and been accused of suggesting baseness," responded Felicia, coldly.

"You spoke under irritation."

"Not at all. I shall be glad to alter my views if you can show better. Tell me your ideas, and I shall be happy to assist you——"

"I know you will, Felicia."

"With any suggestions that may occur to me," Mrs. Walker said, concluding her broken sentence.

"In the first place the furniture and china in Park Lane will have to be sold."

"Sell your furniture! Why all the world would know it in twenty-four hours, and what excuse can you make?"

"The necessity of paying my mother's debts and my own."

If Lady Betty had proposed escaping her creditors by means of the Messieurs Mongolfier's balloon, the notion would not have appeared more preposterous or wildly suicidal to Mrs. Walker.

"Go on, my love," she said, with forced calmness.

"I do not know how much I shall realise by the sale, and I cannot tell the extent of my debts, but I think I shall have more than a hundred pounds when all is settled. I must try and get the matter arranged before I leave London."

"A hundred pounds, and rent and

living at the Wells so expensive. Why, after your dress and journey are paid for, you won't have enough to keep you there six weeks."

Lady Betty had understood that she was to be Felicia's guest during their stay at the waters. She was not displeased to find herself in error; the necessity of keeping up a false position was obviated.

"Then I had better not go," she said, quietly.

"I am entirely of your opinion. If you absolutely insist upon this sale taking place at once you would find it impossible to attend the assemblies, no one would acknowledge you."

The announcement of a visitor put an end to the conversation, much to the satisfaction of both. Lady Betty retired to her room to shed a few tears over the defection of her friend, and made plans for immediate action; while she was still in cogitation a maid brought a packet and placed it in her hands with her mistress's compliments. The packet contained the tradespeople's bills, which Mrs. Walker had not calculated upon finding in less than a month's search.

CHAPTER V.

GERALD TALBOT.

DOCTOR BLANDLY sought Gerard. Leaving Lincoln's Inn he stepped into a hackney coach and instructed the driver to carry him to Brooke's, in St. James's Street, that being, as he took it, the most likely place in which to find him.

"Mr. Crewe isn't here, Sir," said the hall-keeper; "think he must have left town, Sir."

"That is not likely, my good man,"

replied Doctor Blandly, " for he was yesterday in Lincoln's Inn."

" Indeed, Sir, that's particularly odd, Sir, for he wasn't here last night, nor hasn't been for ten days, and a mortal number of members has been asking after him."

" I suppose a gentleman may be in London without of necessity coming to this house?"

" Some gentleman may, Sir, but Mr. Crewe is one of them as can't. I've never known him to stay away two nights running—except when the season's done."

Doctor Blandly returned to his coach and gave the address at which he had met Gerard a fortnight before.

" Is Mr. Gerard Crewe at home ?" he asked of the servant who opened the door.

The servant fetched a card from the

drawer of a table in the passage, and putting it in the Doctor's hands, said:

"Left here a sennight last Saturday. That is his new address."

Once more Doctor Blandly returned to his coach, and, reading the card, told the man to drive him to Cheyne Walk, Chelsea. Stopping before the number indicated, the Doctor looked several times from the house to the card in his hand before he could feel sure that no mistake had been made. The place was dingy and poor, as unlike Gerard's previous dwelling-place as possible.

In answer to his hesitating knock a slatternly girl opened the door, and replying to his inquiry told him to walk up to the second floor, where he would find Mr. Crewe, and warned him to be careful he didn't fall over the breakfast-tray outside the first floor's door.

"The luck has turned," said the Doctor, as he ascended the steep and narrow stairs.

He knocked; Gerard called "Come in;" the Doctor opened the door and stood for a minute unobserved, taking in all that met his eye. It was a small room, one quarter occupied by a four-post bedstead, with two strips of carpet upon the floor. The furniture consisted of three rush-bottomed chairs, a washstand, a chest of drawers, a hanging shelf of books, and a table. The window was open. On the sill stood a long ale glass, with a couple of clove pinks in it—the only gracious thing there. The table was set before the window, and Gerard sat at it, with his back to the door. His chin rested on his left hand; his elbow on the table; in his right hand was a pen; on the table, and at his feet, paper.

Doctor Blandly drew out his snuff-box

mechanically, and tapped it, keeping his eye on the figure before him. At the sound Gerard turned.

"I beg your pardon, Doctor Blandly," he said, rising; "I thought it was my man—I should say, the maid of the house. Be seated, Sir."

He placed a chair to face the window with a nervous glance round the room. Doctor Blandly sat down and slowly took his pinch of snuff.

"Do you snuff, Mr. Talbot?" he asked, extending the box.

A faint flush of colour passed over Gerard's face in being addressed by his father's name.

"Occasionally," he answered, taking from the proffered box and bowing.

"'Tis a boon not to be neglected, Sir. It refreshes the senses and invigorates the mind."

"Is that a recognised fact," Gerard

asked with more anxiety in his tone than the subject seemed to demand.

"It is, Sir—amongst snuff-takers. Perhaps for a young man fresh air and exercise are as effective. Clove-pinks—and very good clove-pinks too," said the Doctor, looking at the flowers, then taking the glass in his hand and examining them more closely, he added—"for London. You are fond of flowers, Sir."

"Who is not?"

"A great many people. People without hearts don't care for them, though let me tell you that your father did not care for them, albeit he had a heart as tender as a child's. By living so long on the sea he relished no colour but blue, and no savour but pitch and saltpetre." The Doctor smelt at the flowers, and said in a tone of encouraging admiration, "Very good clove-pinks. I would have you come and see some that I grow at Edmonton.

They smell sweetest of evenings and early morning; you would give me great pleasure, Sir, to visit me and eat of a fine haunch of mutton that I stuck a skewer into at my butcher's, this morning. I shall have it cooked o' Sunday, if the day will suit you."

"The pleasure will be mine," said Gerard.

"Pleasures are best when shared, Sir. Very good clove-pinks, indeed. Will you put them back in their place? Thank you. You have an agreeable view of the river from this window."

"It compensates the luxuries that you see I possess no longer—or it should. I own I find it difficult at times to reconcile myself to poverty."

"It is hard indeed to change at once the habits that have slowly grown upon us—'tis like the transplanting of a shrub whose roots and fibres have had time to permeate the surrounding soil; for awhile it droops and languishes, its bruised fibres lacking the power to assimilate the strengthening juices of the earth; but anon, Sir, you shall find it strike out with lusty vigour, and flourish with a new and stronger life—especially if the soil be richer."

"Some plants will not bear transplanting, I believe, Doctor."

"'Tis true, Sir, but there are, thank God, not many such of English growth—few indeed, so sappy or so sapless that they will not thrive the better by discreet removal to purer and more wholesome, conditions of existence."

"Shall I be wrong in taking the personal application of your remarks to myself?"

"Certainly not, if the conclusions 1 draw from what I see are correct."

"May I ask you to tell me what those conclusions are?"

"You have turned your back on the

gaming-house, and intend never to return to it—as a gamester."

Gerard listened gravely, and in silence fetched a chair and seated himself by the table opposite his visitor. He looked out upon the river dreamily, and at length ending his meditation with a sigh, turned to Doctor Blandly, and said :

"I am afraid you give me credit for more virtue than I have, Doctor. You do not know that I left the table of necessity."

"You owe nothing, surely."

"No; but my ability to gain is gone."

"You cannot believe in luck to such an extent."

"I never trusted to chance at all. 'Twas that which made me successful. Whilst others were alternately elated and depressed, my temper never varied, and the advantage on my side were enormous. I do not think I am cold by nature ——"

"I am sure you are not," interpellated Doctor Blandly."

"But the circumstances of my life—above all the absence of hope, chilled my blood. I saw nothing in the world to wish for but its luxuries—things that could be bought with money. I knew no friends, no relatives save the villainous foot-pad who called himself my brother, and I owed my position to anonymous charity. With these trammels I could not hope to rise to any state better than that I held. I satisfied my conscience by punctilious honesty in my dealings at the table, and my only ambition by paying back all I had received from you."

"And I wish with all my heart you had kept it."

"Had I never met my brother Tom, I should still be a gamester; but the faculty of centreing my whole thought upon the cards, of maintaining a perfect equanimity under all conditions was weakened on the day he first gave me his hand in friendship; it was destroyed the moment you told me of our relationship. The old fetters were removed, and a new field of hopes and aspirations was opened to me. An intense desire to win a sum of money that would enable me to leave the gaming-table, and learn a profession seized me and ——"

"You lost," said Doctor Blandly, completing the sentence which Gerard had terminated with a shrug. "And a very good job too, Sir. Let me tell you I should be very sorry to see dice on a field vert quartered in the Talbot coat. I should have been better pleased to hear that you relinquished gaming for the honour of your father's name."

"I am a faulty man and not a hero of romance, Doctor Blandly."

"True, Sir, true. The only difference

between you is that you avow the truth, where t'other would be careful to conceal it, and so I give you the preference and my hand, if you will take it."

Gerard gave his hand quickly, and the Doctor grasped it, and held it for a full minute. The wrinkling of his brows showed that his thoughts were busy.

"And so you think of entering a profession with a view to gaining money," he said.

"I am making my first attempt," replied Gerard, with a motion of his hand towards the paper on the table.

"Letters—you have chosen a profession that requires no tedious apprenticeship, like the law or physic. All that you require is patience, a pot of ink—and genius."

"I have the pot of ink," said Gerard, with a laugh.

"And what branch of writing do you affect, Sir?"

"I have begun a comedy."

"I am told it is difficult to get a comedy read."

"I have friends at both houses, and Mr. Kemble has promised me assistance."

"Your mother had excellent dramatic talent, poor soul! A work of this kind should of necessity take a long time to complete, Mr. Talbot."

"I am making but slow progress at present."

Gerard gave a rueful glance at the scattered sheets of erased work, and the few approved lines.

"Do not hurry it, Sir, for the sake of the remuneration you will get by its production. Nature sets us the example of working slowly; nothing that is to last can be done quickly. If you want money I will lend it to you, and you can give no better proof of your friendship than by accepting my service."

"I shall not hesitate to ask you for a loan when I actually need it, Doctor."

"Unfortunately, 'tis the only kind of assistance I can render you, for I lack the imaginative faculty, and I do not profess to have the critical acumen. In physic I might have served you better, but before a fine picture or a good comedy I can only hold up my hands in astonishment and admiration, wondering how the work was done."

"Nevertheless, your opinion and advice would be of service to me. I protest I do not know whether my work is good or bad. I write and re-write again and again, and in the end cannot tell whether the first expression of my thought is better or worse than the last."

"'Tis the diffidence of merit. Only a fool is satisfied with his work, and for him improvement is impossible. When I was a young man, a friend of mine took his first work to Doctor Johnson, and asked him to point out any faults he could find in it. 'Sir,' says Doctor Johnson, ''twill save time to clap the tract on the fire at once, for if you cannot find out the faults for yourself, 'tis because the parts are all faulty alike.'

"Put your manuscript in your pocket and bring it with you on Sunday, Mr. Talbot. You shall read it to me, and have my honest opinion on its merits. I shall judge, not as a critic who hopes to find fault for the exercise of his malicious wit, but as one who takes his place in the pit hoping to be amused."

"I wish I had only your judgment to fear. Unfortunately 'tis the critic and not the audience who decides the fate of a play."

"Well, Sir, you shall have both. I

have a friend in holy orders who shall join us at dinner. He is a man of reading, and preaches excellent sermons, so I am told; I have contracted a vicious habit of sleeping after the Psalms, which prevents me from judging for myself. And now to turn to a sadder subject." The Doctor took a pinch of snuff and then said: "You were at Lincoln's Inn yesterday, I hear."

"No news of my poor brother Tom had been heard."

"None. I was there this morning, and, as you may suppose by my silence, nothing has been heard since your visit respecting your brother Tom. As regards Barnabas Crewe; hitherto he has been represented by a Newgate pettifogger, yesterday he made his appearance at Talbot Hall in person, with his lawyer and half-a-dozen sturdy rogues, who overcame the resistance of the steward and servants, entered the Hall, and there they stay until it is proved that Theophilus Talbot is not the heir. The news was sent this morning by Blake, the steward, who still occupies the lodge and waits for instructions."

"Barnabas must not be allowed to stay there."

"Not a day, Sir, when we can find the means of turning him out. Possession is nine points of the law with such a man as that, and he has a cunning rascal for a lawyer, who, I am afraid, is more than a match for us. He has evidence on his side which we could not overthrow. I might swear that he is Barnabas Crewe until I am black in the face, but at the same time, I must acknowledge that he is identical with the child entered in the parish register as Theophilus Talbot. We have not a single proof that your mother was *enceinte* at the time of her marriage, there is no proof but my word that your father disowned the child. I have only your mother's last words and my own conviction that she was true to your father after her marriage, and that you were his legitimate offspring, which would go for nothing in a court of law. Barnabas is to all effect your brother Tom's heir-at-law."

"Is it impossible to find anyone who knew my mother at the time of her marriage?"

"Your father removed her from her friends in London, thirty years, or nearly thirty years, since. What possibility is there?"

"But little indeed; and yet, from whom did Barnabas get his information? Not from me, certainly, not from you. How could he know the facts which his lawyer has produced except by communicating with one who was intimately acquainted with my father or mother. Depend upon it there is a third person whose existence we have ignored."

The Doctor buried his chin in his hand.

"I can think of no one but his own father," he said, raising his head. "They may have been thrown together by accident; but we could expect no assistance from him, since his own interest would lead him to support his son's claim."

"That makes the case more desperate. Are we to suffer my father's estate to fall into the hands of these two scoundrels? Would not their very looks convict them if they stood before a judge?"

"Not if blushes were needed as a proof of guilt. I am strongly opposed to making this misfortune public, though if you wish it I will give you all the support in my power. In the first place, it could not result in benefit to you."

"You do not think I have any motive but the honour of my family?"

"No, and that is a reason for avoiding publicity. If you failed to prove your case, Barnabas would be recognised as legitimate, and the line of the Talbots would include a wretch whom we know to be a highwayman, whom I suspect to be a murderer."

"Great Heavens! do you suspect him of murdering Tom?"

"Who else could have so strong a motive, if, as we suppose, he knew beforehand of the relationship between them?"

"You think that Barnabas murdered Tom?" asked Gerard, coldly.

"I do," the Doctor replied, thinking only of the evidence.

The blood rushed into Gerard's face, and he dropped his face into his hands.

"My mother's son," he said, with a groan.

"What have I said?" the Doctor cried, springing to his feet. "Pardon me, my boy. I can think of you only as Tom's brother. Don't take my words to heart. 'Twas an idle suspicion that escaped me in an unguarded moment."

"No idle suspicion," Gerard said, dropping his hands between his knees, without raising his head. "'Tis a fact which I should have suspected, but that the crime was too horrible to attribute to my brother. Barnabas a murderer—'twas shame enough to know him as a thief. *My* brother a murderer—'tis an encouraging reflection to begin the new life with—a passport to decent society—an advantage which critics would not fail to mention amongst the merits of my work—a charm to win the affections of a cultured girl."

"And a stimulant to courage, Gerard," added the Doctor. "So that you are free from blame, why should you heed prejudice. Your father was best pleased when the sea was crowded with enemies, for there was the greatest prospect of glory for his King. Let your conscience be your king; fight a good fight for its honour, and never fear what may happen. The good opinion of four honest men—nay, your own satisfaction alone—outweighs a thousand times the flattery of a crowd of fools."

"Can we do nothing to free my father's name from the disgrace that this scoundrel throws upon it? If he got into the Hall with the aid of a dozen men, can't we turn him out with the aid of a dozen more?"

"A useless game of Crambo that we should lose by. No. Take my advice—leave him alone. His own actions will prove to all thinking people that he is not your father's son, but a rascally imposter. He will be shunned by everyone; and his life at Talbot Hall will not be too cheerful, I engage. I have a flea for his ear that will make him heartily repent his knavery. I am heartily mistaken if before the end of twelve months he does not offer to make a public renunciation of his rights for a few hundred pounds down."

"What power have you? He has the Hall."

"And I have the money." The Doctor took out his snuff-box, and gave it a tap of satisfaction. "And rather than let a penny of it go into his hands, I'll squander it all in the Court of Chancery. He can't pay his expenses, and his lawyer will not undertake a game at which he must in the end lose. He may kill a few head of deer, and shoot as much game as

he likes—let him. There will still be
enough for us to celebrate his departure
when his time comes. He may empty the
cellar, and probably will in a few weeks—
let him again, I say. Thank heaven
there's a cave full of port and Burgundy
that is known to no one but me—now that
poor Tom's gone. As for the rents of
the property, my man in Lincoln's Inn
will get an injunction to stop him from
receiving a mag. He shan't cut a single
one of those blessed old oaks in the park.
Without money he will get no one to serve
him; without wine he will get no one, not
even his fellow rogues, to visit him. He
won't be able to get powder and shot to
kill his own game—take a pinch, Mr.
Talbot—and if he can sleep alone in that
empty Hall, with no liquor to stupify his
senses, he is not the man I take him to be.
Twelve months—why I won't give him six
months lease of his ill-gotten home. We

shall have him whining at our feet for mercy and pardon before Christmas is upon us, Sir."

CHAPTER VI.

THE TAMING OF MRS. BAXTER.

"Park Lane, August 1, 1800.

"DEAR Doctor Blandly,
"I should be wanting in due appreciation of your kindness if I failed to ask your guidance through the difficulty which besets me at the present moment. With the permission of Mrs. Walker, I have abandoned my intention of spending a season at the Wells, and I wish to arrange my pecuniary affairs, and enter upon those duties which my altered position necessitates at once. I have collected my dear mother's

bills, and find that my liabilities amount to the sum of four hundred and seventy pounds seventeen shilings; this with the sum owing to Mr. Moss reaches a total of seven hundred and seventy pounds seventeen shillings. I have in my purse nearly one hundred and ninety-seven pounds, and that with the proceeds arising from the sale of the furniture, &c., in the house will be, I hope, more than sufficient to pay all I owe, including the rent of the house.

"But I do not know any gentleman in the auctioneering trade, and so I ask you to tell me what course I shall take for the disposal of the china and things. I have had everything well brushed and polished, and save my clothes and a work-box which was poor dear mamma's, all packed in two trunks, and an elbow-chair which is set aside in the garret, everything is ready to be sold, and may be seen by applying to me, or to the person in charge of the house if I am absent.

"With sincere gratitude for your goodness to me and my poor mother,

"I am, dear Doctor Blandly,

"Obediently yours,

"Elizabeth St. Cyr."

Doctor Blandly read this letter, which he found beside "The Times" newspaper on his table when he came in from making the tour of his garden, which was his custom, in fair or foul weather, before sitting down to his breakfast.

"A very good letter, and well writ," he said, holding the sheet at arm's length, and looking at the even lines and bold characters with a kindly critical eye. 'Neatly folded, well expressed, and every line of it the unstudied product of a clear and healthy mind—so I take it." He read it again, commenting as he went.

"Beset with difficulties—aye, aye, you have need of a pilot, poor child—thrown like a frail skiff into the hurrying current of the work-a-day world, where be abundance of hard rocks and few placid pools! .... So Mrs. Walker has permitted you to go your own way. One understands that. 'Tis well for you, Miss Betty, though I wager your heart ached to find her so fickle a friend .... Duties—duties? Ha, yes, the duty of living frugally upon her slender means. .... She's more anxious to discharge her debts than to make a profit for herself —a good girl. .... Don't know any gentleman in the auctioneering trade—no, nor I, my dear; nevertheless we must content ourselves with such as we have. .... Two trunks and an elbow-chair set aside in the garret—a chair too old to sell perhaps; and is that all the furniture she reserves for her new home. Everything ready to be sold—that means much—the selling of all that is dear by usage and familiarity, yet not a word of the pain it costs to part with them. I can fancy the child polishing those trifles for the last time, and bravely staunching her tears the while. 'Tis a brave girl—and her brief, clear letter is more touching than if it were filled with regrets and blotted with tears—a good, brave girl."

Doctor Blandly laid down the letter and took up the "Times," as if to divert his thoughts from the subject until he could think of it with less emotion. As his eyes wandered down the columns of the paper they fell upon this advertisement:

"A Young Lady desires an engagement in a family or school, to teach young children. Address, Miss St. Cyr, Park Lane, London."

"What!" he cried, "she is prepared to work for a livelihood, and submit to the tyranny of a jealous mother, or a grasping school-mistress, for a pittance scarcely sufficient to buy clothes to her back, rather than accept my protection and help ! By George, she's a trump of a girl ! "

He sat in cogitation for some time, looking now at the letter and then at the advertisement, and again at his slowly twiddling thumbs. Finally he rose from his seat and rang the bell.

"Bring me my Sunday coat and shoes, Jerry," said he, when the old servant appeared :

" Your Sunday coat and shoes, or your fishing coat and shoes, Sir ?"

" Do I look as if I were going a-fishing."

Jerry looked in his master's face, and finding not a particle of pleasure in its expression, withdrew without asking for further confirmation.

Doctor Blandly walked over to the Vicarage.

A pastor in a garden, surrounded by his children, ought to be a subject worthy of a painter, but the Reverend John Baxter, under similar conditions, was a subject deserving rather the practical sympathy of the philanthropist. Jane, his youngest daughter, was cutting her teeth, and had to be nursed; little Anne was quietly making herself ill, and staining her clean bib, with mulberries; and the two boys, in open rebellion against their father, refused to study their primer, and dodged him amongst the gooseberry bushes when he sought to bring them to obedience. The weather was sultry, the Reverend John Baxter was stout, and more than once in his pursuit the straggling branches of the prickly gooseberry laid hold of his ungaitered legs, causing him to stumble violently, to the mortal jeopardy of the screaming babe in his arms. It was just as he had relinquished the chase for a minute to go and tear little Anne away from the mulberries that he caught sight of Doctor Blandly on the other side of the privet hedge, making his way towards the vicarage.

Abandoning his child in the greater danger which awaited his friend, Mr. Baxter moved towards the privet hedge to warn his friend off, but Doctor Blandly was already in the garden, and close to the door of the house. In vain he waved his arm as a signal to retreat, and shaped with his mouth the words, "Don't; for the love of heaven, don't! *She's at home!*" The Doctor was deep in thought, and never averted his eye from the path before him until he had knocked at the door of the vicarage.

Mrs. Baxter herself opened the door. She had a pen in her hand, and a tart expression on her face.

"You have come to see Mr. Baxter, I presume," said the lady, frigidly.

"No, madam, I have come to see you. If you can give me five minutes' attention I will explain my business."

"Business! Baxter has not told me a word of it."

"Baxter did not know, madam; so 'twas not his fault that you did not know, nor yours neither," he added, in an undertone.

Mrs. Baxter led the Doctor into a grim chamber, where a number of parochial books and papers showed that she was managing her husband's business.

Doctor Blandly seated himself on an angular, narrow chair, with a slipping horse-hair seat, and came to the point without waste of time.

"Mrs. Baxter," said he, "I hear you have lost your governess."

"I sent her away at a minute's notice for impertinence."

"Poor soul!"

"Oh, of course, you pity *her*, Doctor Blandly."

"On the contrary, ma'am, 'tis you that I pity. The young woman has, in all probability, found another engagement more suitable to her disposition, whereas you are still without a governess for your children, which must of necessity give you less time to devote to your husband's affairs. Will you be good enough to look at this advertisement, which I have cut from the 'Times' newspaper of this morning."

Mrs. Baxter took the cutting, and drawing down the corners of her thin lips in anticipation, read it through.

"I see nothing attractive in *that*," she remarked; "a *young lady* wishes for an engagement. Governesses are coming to something, indeed! *Young person* would have been more respectful. Not a word about accomplishments."

"She possibly thought it unnecessary to talk of accomplishments, as she wishes to teach young children."

"Ah, that again—her wish to teach young children is an evidence of incapacity."

"Had she advertised to teach elder children, I should not have thought it worth while to show you the advertisement."

"*Miss* St. Cyr. I should have thought initials, or her christian name alone, more appropriate. She does not mention the name of her mistress, which is, in my opinion, a flagrant outrage upon propriety, as the lady lives in Park Lane."

"Miss St. Cyr has no mistress, and the address given is her own house."

"Impossible!"

"Not at all. She is an orphan, and the whole of her fortune was lost through an unfortunate investment which I made with her mother's capital shortly before her death, which happened in May last."

"I have not heard a word of this from Baxter."

"For certain reasons, madam, I do not tell Baxter all that I do and know."

Mrs. Baxter read the advertisement again, and her lips instead of being drawn down towards her chin, were now stretched back in a horizontal line towards her ears.

"Her modesty is certainly becoming," she said, "and 'twould be a great advantage for Samuel and Luke to be instructed by a refined young lady. Under their father's training they have grown so violent, that I find it difficult myself to command respect. Little Anne can walk alone, and 'tis high time she learnt a hymn, and Jane is very fractious of nights."

"If you read the advertisement again, you will see that Miss St. Cyr does not undertake to do the work of a nurse."

Mrs. Baxter drew up her mobile lips into the resemblance of a bladder-neck at this reminder, and then shaking her head said,

"I do not as a rule employ unfortunate people; they are generally undeserving, and frequently expect indulgence, instead of showing that active anxiety to give satisfaction, which their humbled condition should prompt. Still they are more ready to accept moderate terms of remuneration than people of greater experience."

"As concerns remuneration, Mrs. Baxter, I have a suggestion to make, which I hope will not be unacceptable. I wish you to give Miss St. Cyr whatever terms she asks without abatement, and in addition, I wish her to be provided with all the comforts you would offer her were the young lady merely a guest in your house. If a nursemaid to soothe the temper of your infant will make the house more agreeable as a home to the young lady, by all means engage a nursemaid. Whatever expenses these alterations in your establishment may oblige, I will discharge, on the condition that the financial arrangement shall be absolutely a secret between you and me."

"Oh, of course, Doctor Blandly. But I really do not know how to——" Mrs. Baxter hesitated, but a greedy hungriness overspread her face, and showed that she was well-disposed to receive the Doctor's proposal.

"You shall reckon up your expenses at the end of each week or month as you choose, and I will pay them *without asking any questions.*"

Mrs. Baxter's stony eyes fell, and she

stroked her nose with the end of her pen in some confusion; but the prize was too good to be sacrificed to modesty.

"If 'tis an act of charity, Doctor——"

"No 'tis no charity, but simply a very poor restitution on my part."

"In that case I need not hesitate. I will write at once, though I'm afraid I have nothing but business paper. I promise the young lady shall be treated with all due consideration and attention."

"Very well, madam," said Doctor Blandly, rising; "and so long as she is satisfied to stay with you, I will provide funds."

With a few more words Doctor Blandly closed the interview, and then left the Vicarage. Mrs. Baxter at once wrote a note requesting the pleasure of an interview with Miss St. Cyr, at her "earliest convenience," and despatched the sexton on the Reverend John Baxter's cob, with instructions to give the note into Miss St. Cyr's own hand. Doctor Blandly also wrote to Lady Betty, expressing his approval of the determination she had come to, and informing her that his lawyer in Lincoln's Inn would wait upon her, and make all necessary arrangements for the sale of her furniture, and the payment of her debts.

CHAPTER VII.

LADY BETTY'S VISIT.

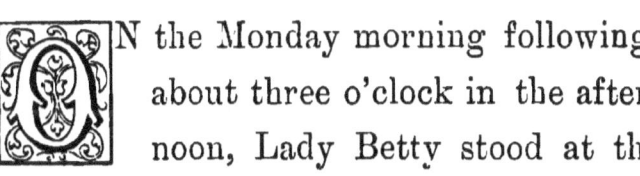N the Monday morning following, about three o'clock in the afternoon, Lady Betty stood at the gate of Dr. Blandly's garden. Jerry had instructions to admit without delay a young lady dressed in black, whenever she came, and to treat her with as much respect as if she were a gentleman; so he answered her question with a low bow, saying in his most polite tones, that Doctor Blandly was at home, and begged her to follow him.

Lady Betty passed through the wicket by the side of the house, and coming upon a full view of the garden, which was ablaze with free growing annuals, geraniums, fuchsias and hollyhocks she stopped for a moment while her being seemed to expand as she imbibed the delicious colour and fragrance around her. It was the first time she had stood in a garden since the autumn holidays at Winchmore, a year ago. Her heart wept and smiled, as happy memories and sad passed through her mind.

"Oh, if I could only hope," she sighed, "or if I might lay aside my mourning clothes, and wear light muslin, and sit in the shade watching the bees, and feasting my senses like them, without regret—with nothing but lazy indifference!"

"If you please, miss," said Jerry, coming back to her side across the lawn, treading the gravel on the points of his toes, and speaking in a whisper, "master is asleep." He pointed over the flowerbeds to the apple-tree in the middle of the lawn, under which the Doctor sat.

"I will walk about the garden until he wakes," said Lady Betty.

"Thank you, miss; the weather's so hot, and he do like his doze after lunch to that extent, that I can't abear to wake him. Can I bring you anything, miss? A bottle of claret, now—the port I shouldn't recommend before dinner."

"No, thank you. If I want refreshment I will find some fruit."

Jerry scratched his ear, and said with more hesitation—

"Master wouldn't begrudge the best wine there is in the cellar, but he's that perticlar about his wall-fruit, that I daren't so much as pick up a dropped plum when it's green."

"I will spare the wall-fruit," Lady Betty said, smiling.

With many thanks for her consideration, and as many bows, old Jerry retired to the cellar where he had bottling on hand; and Lady Betty taking the shady path, walked slowly down the garden, stooping now and then to pick the flowers which were her favourites. After a while she crossed the lawn to the apple-tree, and sat upon the seat which surrounded it. Doctor Blandly was not upon this seat, but comfortably settled in his cushioned Windsor-chair. He wore a pair of nankeen-breeches, thin stockings, and a coat and waistcoat of white jean; his head and face were veiled with the yellow India handkerchief. His feet were crossed, and his hands were folded in his lap; a table was at his right hand, on which were disposed an ale glass, a long clay pipe, a pruning knife, and a volume of Cowper's Poems. These things told the character of the man.

Lady Betty sat arranging the flowers she had gathered, content with her occupation and an occasional look at the blue sky through the foliage of the apple-tree, and the coloured beds that skirted the lawn. Presently the Doctor drew a long breath, knitted his finger-tips and slowly twiddled his thumbs. Then in a low voice he sang:

> " This little old 'oman, so I've heered tell,
> She went to market her eggs for to sell
> Singing, tol de rol, de rol, and a hi tol de rol."

Lady Betty gave the softest "ahem!" Doctor Blandly pulled down his handkerchief.

"Bless my soul, Miss Betty!" he cried, catching sight of the young lady before him, who, with a little smile on her pretty pale face, and her head on one side, was regarding the bouquet she had made. "Why didn't that fool of a Jerry wake me?"

"Because he is a good servant, and fond of his master. I have not been here long, and not a moment has seemed too long."

"You are tired with your journey. Dear heart! to think I should be asleep! Jerry!"

"I am not at all tired. I have only walked from the Vicarage, where Mrs. Baxter insisted upon my taking lunch."

"The Vicarage!" exclaimed Doctor Blandly, with feigned surprise, at the same time stooping to pick up his straw hat and conceal the expression on his face. "Now what on earth could have taken you there, Miss Betty?"

"Mrs. Baxter saw an advertisement I had printed in the 'Times' newspaper, and wrote to me on Friday to engage me as a governess for her children."

"Lord, ah! Baxter said something about his wife losing her governess, now

I come to think of it. But what a strange coincidence that she should write to you. I give you my word I never mentioned your name to *him*. Well, my dear, I hope you have accepted the engagement, for then you will have one friend to come to see now and then."

" I have accepted, and I think I shall begin the new life on Saturdry next."

" I'm downright glad to hear it. Mrs. Baxter and I don't get on well together, but that is an advantage in one respect; when you want to escape from her you can come here without fear of being followed. Baxter's a good, soft, stupid old soul, you'll like him." He took his pruning-knife, and rising from his chair, said, with a look of much promise, " Come with me, my dear." He gave her his hand to rise, and held it in his as they walked slowly over the lawn towards the sunny wall.

"You're a brave girl," he said to her, in a low, emphatic tone, "a good brave girl! Your sorrows have come early, but if we must love and lose, 'tis better to suffer while the heart is young and vigorous. Buds nipped in the spring are not missed in the summer, but nothing replaces the autumn loss, and the old stock may not bear another bloom."

Lady Betty glanced at the Doctor's face, and her eyes filled with tears, not for herself, but for him. The tone of his voice, the far-away look in his face, told her that it was not a mere sentimental generality he had uttered, but the summary of his own experience. She held his hand a little tighter, and did not break the reverie into which he seemed to have fallen. She would have been content to walk in silence for an indefinite time, united by hand and heart in a bond of sympathy, but they came face to face with the peaches, and Doctor Blandly's thoughts returned from the past to the present, from the passion that was dead to the love that lived.

"There's a jolly fellow!" said he, turning back a leaf to expose a velvety fruit; "but he will be better to cut to-morrow about eleven, another afternoon's sun, and the mellowing influence of the night air, is wanted to make him perfect. Now down here there's a chap that I ought to have culled this morning, but I couldn't, he looked so comfortable and happy." He led the way down the path, still holding Lady Betty by the hand, towards the "chap" in question; but he stopped to gently lift a peach from the naked brick to the tenderer surface of a leaf, saying as he did so: "Ha! ha! my boy! you will rub your cheek against that wall, will you?"

When they came to the ripe favourite,

he paused for a minute or two to point out its excellent points to Lady Betty, and then planting one foot on the path and the other across the bed against the wall, he opened his knife and cut it from the stem with as much care as if the life of the tree were at stake. He placed the fruit in Lady Betty's hand, and went on to gather another and another until he had collected six, and with these they returned to the shadow of the apple-tree. At the same moment Jerry came from the house with a bottle and glasses.

"I've come upon a bottle of the green-waxed Madeiry, master," said he.

"Do you like Madeira, Miss Betty, or do you prefer the red wine?" asked the Doctor.

Lady Betty expressed her satisfaction with Madeira, and the Doctor poured out the wine, after carefully examining the condition of the glasses.

"Perhaps the young lady would like a little Burgundy in about twenty minutes," suggested Jerry.

"When we want more I will call you, Jerry," said the Doctor, and then added in an undertone: "Tell your wife to come and present her duty presently, and, Jerry," as that servant was withdrawing with comprehensive winks, "put about half a shovelful of manure down against the roots of that crinkley peach at once."

Lady Betty found the fruit worthy of all Doctor Blandly had said in its commendation, but could with difficulty convince him that two were sufficient to satisfy her appetite. That she might not lose any particle of the flavour by other considerations, the Doctor limited his conversation to peaches during the feast, and the stock of his comment upon that fruit were yet unexhausted when Jerry's wife, a neat spare woman of fifty or thereabouts, in her best cap and a clean apron, came down to the apple-tree to present her duty.

"Miss Betty," said Doctor Blandly, "this is Kate, Jerry's wife. Kate, this is Miss Betty St. Cyr, of whom I have spoken."

"You will find me most obedient and dutiful, Miss," said Kate, with a bob.

"And now, my dear, if you will follow Kate, she will show you your room, and get you anything you lack."

"Thank you, Doctor Blandly, I cannot stay."

"Not stay, my dear!" exclaimed the Doctor, with dejection. "There's a cold haunch of mutton that's as short as venison, that with a pickled walnut——"

"And the damson pie made a purpose," added Kate. Lady Betty opened her eyes.

"The fact is," said the Doctor, in confusion. "I had a sort of impression, a kind of prediction that you would come to-day. You promised to visit me you know."

"I am, indeed sorry that I cannot stay. I have fixed six o'clock this evening for an interview at my house with the lawyer."

"Well, my dear—business must be minded, but I am disappointed. However, you are to be my neighbour, and opportunities will not be wanting of tasting Kate's excellent pies. Kate, you can go."

Kate made a bob, and with a few "dootiful words," retired.

"Shall you return by the coach?" asked Doctor Blandly.

"Yes—if I can find a place."

"Jerry shall secure that for you. There is a coach leaves the 'Angel' at four, which will set you down at Hyde Park

Corner. Had I been sure of your coming and suspected that you would leave so soon, I would certainly have retained a friend of yours who left me this morning, to accompany you."

"A friend of mine?"

"Gerard." The Doctor watched the expression of Lady Betty's face to see what effect the name made upon her. Her cheek remained untinged with colour."

"Mr. Crewe?"

"No, not Mr. Crewe—but your friend, Gerard still. When did you see him last?"

"He came to take me for a drive on Thursday, in his Clarence."

"In *his* Clarence?"

"I am not sure that it was his. It was certainly not the one he usually uses— but he keeps a Clarence. Does that surprise you?"

The Doctor drew a long breath; then he smacked his thigh, and giving his head a toss, cried:

"Well done, Gerard! You young people have the courage of the—hum! of St. George himself. Poor boy—so he took you for a drive in a Clarence! And I'll be bound he said never a word of his altered condition."

"N—o—o," Lady Betty replied, opening her eyes wider and wider. "What is the mystery—why is he Gerard and not Mr. Crewe, and why are you so astonished that he took me for a drive?"

"Because on Thursday morning I found him lodged in a garret with nothing but a pennyworth of clove-pinks to compensate him for all the luxuries he has lost. Surprised—no; now I know him I am not surprised at what he did to give you pleasure. 'Twas not a miserable pride that made him conceal his poverty, but the fear that the knowledge would prevent you accepting his services. Surprised!" The Doctor exclaimed giving his thigh another slap—"not a bit of it. He is a Talbot."

"Talbot!" cried Lady Betty, catching his arm with trembling eager fingers—"Talbot?"

"Yes, he is our poor Tom's brother!"

"And he is quite poor?"

"Yes, poor as a poet. He has given up his fashionable trade, because it was not fit for an honest gentleman, and because the honour of his family rests upon him."

"How can he be poor and Tom's brother."

"Tom never knew of the relationship."

"Ah! I understand—but ——"

"Why does he not inherit his brother's estate you ask. My dear, these are circumstances which I cannot tell you. Tom was the son of Admiral Talbot's first wife; Gerard, the son of the second; but between them a third person was born, who was not the Admiral's son, and he unfortunately, usurps a claim which cannot be contested."

" I do not want to know that. Gerard is poor, and he spent money that he could ill-afford to give his brother's sweetheart pleasure."

" You need not regret it, Miss Betty," the Doctor said, seeing the tear in her eye.

" Regret it, no ! I rejoice in it. Tom would have done that, but no man else except his brother !"

" They are gentlemen—English gentlemen to the marrow, Miss Betty !"

"And what is Mr. ——, what is Gerard —Gerard Talbot doing in his poor garret ?"

" What usually is done in a garret—he

is writing a comedy. He brought a few pages in his pocket yesterday, and I assure you 'tis prodigious fine. I wanted my friend Baxter, to hear 'em read, but the poor man couldn't be spared. However, I have bound Gerard to come every Sunday, and read his week's work after dinner until the five acts are finished. And you shall come on Sundays, and so shall Baxter, and we will listen to the man's work, and give him our poor help, if we see right to advise. What say you to that, Miss Betty?"

Lady Betty's eyes glowed with pleasure. She longed to look at Gerard in the new character he bore to her.

"He is my brother—as much as though the parson had married me to Tom," she cried.

"Well, well," said the Doctor, taking out his snuff-box. "We shall see about that. At any rate, you agree to dine with us next Sunday, and every Sunday after, don't you, my dear?"

"Oh, yes—that is ——" Lady Betty's face lengthened. "I am only a governess, and Mrs. Baxter ——"

"Oh! I'll settle her—that is, Baxter will arrange all that. He has a wonderful influence over his wife has Baxter."

"I shall be happy—very happy to come and listen to his voice. I thank you very much for the kindness in thinking of me—and Doctor Blandly ——"

"Well, my dear."

"Do you mind my sending the elbow chair here?"

"Send it by all means. Is it the chair you mentioned in your letter?"

"Yes—I couldn't sell it, and I do not want to take it amongst strange people."

"Let me have it. It shall be taken care of whatever it is."

The Reverend John Baxter, with tears in his eyes, said that he had promised to explain Bunyan's "Holy War" to his children, and could not escape.

"Very well then, you will come the Sunday following," said the Doctor, in a tone of irritation.

The Vicar looked at his wife for permission, but that lady stood with her arms folded one upon the other below her spare bosom, her nostrils pinched, her lips hermetically closed, and her stony eyes fixed on vacancy—the very picture of indifference.

"Mrs. Baxter said you are to do as you choose," cried the Doctor; "unless you doubt the truth of her assertion, which would be unpardonable, you will follow your own wishes; and if you do not come I shall take your refusal as a direct affront."

Baxter plucked up courage, and in a

faltering voice accepted the Doctor's invitation.

In consequence of this arrangement, Doctor Blandly begged Gerard to defer the reading of his work for a week, which he willingly agreed to do, for as yet he was not proud of his work, and very much preferred devoting his thoughts to Lady Betty than to his comedy.

He was astonished by the change he found in her. She had never been to him so softly sweet and charming. She was at the house when he arrived, and ran down the steps and across the grass-plot to meet him. She called him Gerard for the first time, as she held his hand and looked up into his face with wide, melting eyes. She pressed him to take refreshment after the fatigue of his journey. She seemed nervously happy, like a child in the presence of a long-expected friend.

She listened eagerly to everything he said, smiled when he smiled, was gravely anxious when he spoke of the difficulties attending the work he had undertaken; he felt that her eyes were fixed upon him when he was speaking to Doctor Blandly. As they sat under the apple-tree, she with a lapfull of flowers which she was making up into bouquets for the decoration of Doctor Blandly's chimney-piece, it was his taste she consulted first in the selection, his approval she demanded. Now and then she looked up from her occupation to his face, and returned to it with a smile.

Was the happiness due to the natural surroundings of flower and verdure, or to his having entered the field of literature, Gerard asked himself.

After doing full justice to the excellent damson pie Kate had prepared for the occasion, Doctor Blandley, despite his endeavours to keep awake, dropped into a doze, seated in his Windsor chair; then Lady Betty proposed a walk in the shady side of the garden. She slipped her hand under Gerard's arm, and was first to break the silence which a mutual happiness had produced.

"I know all, Gerard," she said softly.

"All, Lady Betty?"

"All that Doctor Blandly thought fit for me to know—all that I want to know. You are poor dear Tom's brother, and since I am his widow—for indeed our hearts were one—you are my brother also. We are not quite alone in the world, you and I—we have lost and we have found. And you are glad to have me for a sister, aren't you?"

"I did not expect to gain so much of your affection."

"But you loved me, all the same. You said to yourself, 'There's my poor little sister all alone in the dismal house in Park Lane; she has no one to comfort her, no one to take her away from herself,' and you saved up your money, though you were horribly poor, to hire a carriage for my use. And while I still regarded you as a stranger, and looked upon your generous kindness as a mere act of gallantry, you felt towards me as I feel towards you now."

"Doctor Blandly has told you more than he should."

"Not one word, Gerard, for he knew 'twould make me happy, and lessen my grief. And, besides, should there be any secrets between us, who are so near to each other. There is nothing I would conceal from you. I have made up my mind to tell you every Sunday when we meet all that has happened during the week, just as a sister should tell her brother. I have quite a great deal to tell you about my new engagement. Poor Mr. Baxter is quite a martyr; his bread is buttered for him like the children's, and Mrs. Baxter is a tyrant—though she is excessively gracious to me, and would make me ill with good things if she could—but she *is* a tyrant for all that, and she has a mouth like this—look."

" A pretty mouth then under the most adverse conditions," said Gerard, regarding the little *moue* Lady Betty made with her soft, pretty lips.

" Even a brother's compliment must be acknowledged," said Lady Betty, making a mock courtesy. She was gay with excitement; and again taking Gerard's arm, she continued : " Of course I cannot tell you much yet—for I only took my ' situation ' yesterday; but I shall keep a diary, and you shall see it if you like when we meet on Sundays. The boys, my pupils, are dreadful children; they kick their father's shins when their sister all alone in the dismal house in Park Lane; she has no one to comfort her, no one to take her away from herself,' and you saved up your money, though you were horribly poor, to hire a carriage for my use. And while I still regarded you as a stranger, and looked upon your generous kindness as a mere act of gallantry, you felt towards me as I feel towards you now."

"Doctor Blandly has told you more than he should."

"Not one word, Gerard, for he knew 'twould make me happy, and lessen my grief. And, besides, should there be any secrets between us, who are so near to each other. There is nothing I would conceal from you. I have made up my mind to tell you every Sunday when we meet all that has happened during the week, just as a sister should tell her brother. I have quite a great deal to tell you about my new engagement. Poor Mr. Baxter is

quite a martyr; his bread is buttered for
him like the children's, and Mrs. Baxter
is a tyrant—though she is excessively
gracious to me, and would make me ill
with good things if she could—but she *is*
a tyrant for all that, and she has a mouth
like this—look."

" A pretty mouth then under the most
adverse conditions," said Gerard, regarding the little *moue* Lady Betty made with
her soft, pretty lips.

" Even a brother's compliment must be
acknowledged," said Lady Betty, making
a mock courtesy. She was gay with excitement; and again taking Gerard's arm,
she continued : " Of course I cannot tell
you much yet—for I only took my ' situation' yesterday; but I shall keep a
diary, and you shall see it if you like
when we meet on Sundays. The boys,
my pupils, are dreadful children; they
kick their father's shins when their

mother's back is turned. I have made them understand that they will have to treat me with more respect, or they will form the subject of an additional chapter to Fox's 'Book of Martyrs.' I pity poor Mr. Baxter this afternoon, he has to interest them with an explanation of Bunyan's 'Holy War.' I could never understand it, could you?"

"I don't think that I ever attempted to."

"I used to love the 'Pilgrim's Progress' until I was told it was a kind of riddle with a moral answer to it." Lady Betty paused, possibly to take breath, and after a moment's silence, she said, giving Gerard's arm a little pinch:

"I am so glad you are writing a comedy, Gerard."

"You prefer a poor poet to a wealthy gamester?"

"That depends. Poets as a rule are

rather ridiculous, whereas there is a dash and spirit about gamesters that recommend them to my taste. I do like courage, even when it is not quite what folks call ' proper.' "

"There is no courage in playing with the assurance of winning, and a gamester who plays for his living must have that assurance."

"That is true. 'Tis, perhaps, simply because the gamester wears a better coat that girls prefer him to the poet. Men are guided by what they think, we girls by what we see, I believe."

"Would you have liked me equally had I remained a gamester?"

"Oh, no; you wouldn't have seemed to me like a brother of Tom's if you had done that which he would have scorned to do. And I couldn't have felt so proud of you if you had not accepted poverty for the honour of your name."

" Still you do not care for poets."

" Not those who write elegant lines and are always rhyming anguish and languish, and hearts and darts. Oh, I hate the name of Phyllis! Those poets are very different to men who can write plays. How many acts shall you have in your comedy?"

" Five."

" I hope they will be good long acts."

" You are not afraid that your patience will be exhausted?"

" Oh, no; I am always sorry when a play is over, and I shall be ready to cry when the irritable old father is at length forced to give his consent to the marriage of the young people, and the servants and friends drop in and begin to form a semi-circle at the back of the principal characters."

" But supposing I end my comedy in a different manner?"

"*Can* you, Gerard?" asked Lady Betty, in grave doubt.

"I think so."

"You must be clever."

"That remains to be seen. I have doubts."

"I have none," cried Lady Betty, firmly. "A man who can do admirable things must be able to write them. When do you think you shall finish your comedy?"

"By the end of the year, I hope."

"There are a great many Sundays before then, and you will read all that you have done every week. That will be lovely. And afterwards it will be played at the theatre."

"If the manager does not reject it."

"Oh, he cannot be so stupid as all that. Doctor Blandly and I will have a side-box all to ourselves, and get there the moment the doors open, and I shall be dreadfully impatient until the curtain goes up, but all the same I wouldn't miss a moment of the time; and then, when the curtain drops, I will clap. It may not be genteel, but I'll clap with all my might. I should like Mr. and Mrs. Baxter and the children to be somewhere in the house where I could see them—not in the same box with me. I should not have patience with them, they would seem so commonplace and vulgar. How those boys would clap if I promised them something—or if their father told them not to. And then, when the five acts were played, all the audience would insist upon your coming forward on the stage, and then I shouldn't be able to see you for crying."

The girl's eyes were tearful in anticipation of such joy, and Gerard, looking down upon her sensitive, sweet face, felt that there was a stronger incentive to struggle for success than poverty.

"Dear heart o' me!" exclaimed the Doctor, opening his eyes about this time, " I declare I must have lost consciousness for half a minute. Where are the young people? I must make my excuses to them for my want of manners."

He jumped up, and catching sight of their figures through the hollyhocks, crossed the lawn briskly in that direction. Suddenly he paused. They had their backs towards him, walking leisurely down the path, Lady Betty leaning on Gerard's arm, he looking down upon her face.

The Doctor took out his snuff-box, planted his feet a foot asunder, set his head on one side, and, slowly smoothing the lid of his box with the ball of his thumb, said to himself, " The child loves him for being the brother of her dead lover; but the end of loving him for the sake of another will probably be that she will love him for himself, thinking more of him as another fades from her memory."

Then the Doctor took his pinch, which seemed to give him much satisfaction.

CHAPTER IX.

IN TOM'S PLACE.

LADY BETTY hailed the returning Sunday with a feeling of intense satisfaction. The occupation of the week had not distressed her—had not been half so unpleasant as she expected. The children had distracted her thoughts, and made her forget her troubles for the greater part of the day. But she did not wish to forget: it seemed to her like the neglect of an affectionate duty to give so little of her time to the memory of Tom. The vague religious teaching she had received led her to imagine that his immortal spirit was cognisant of all she did, and she feared to grieve him by neglect. She did not think of his sensitive jealousy as a mortal weakness.

She longed for a day to devote to him; to kneel in church and worship God and holy things with his unseen essence by her side. After the service she would go home with Doctor Blandly, and there meet Gerard, in whom she found, or fancied that she found, a hundred points of resemblance to her dead lover, and who was united to her by sympathy and an affinity of misfortune.

Mrs. Baxter's religion was of another kind, and Sunday was, of course, a day of penance. From the moment she rose she spoke in a low, sepulchral voice, as if some one lay dead in the house. She walked slowly and firmly, moving like an engine at half speed. She made the chocolate weaker than usual, and substituted dry toast for the customary dish of bacon. Half an hour before it was necessary she arrayed herself in the most hearse-like costume, a sable plume in her beaver bonnet, and a black velvet pall over her shoulders, and sat in the sitting-room issuing orders to the servant-maid in the kitchen without moving her head or a muscle of her limbs. The moment that the church bell commenced to call folks to church she summoned Baxter, and having inspected him from the top of his wig to the tag of his shoe-string, to assure herself that he was in a creditable state, she took his arm and led him off to the church.

Lady Betty followed with the two boys, Samuel and Luke, and took them with her into the vicar's family pew, while Mrs. Baxter, having cast a sharp eye round the empty church to see that the pew-opener had neglected none of his duties, conducted her husband into the vestry to give him the finishing touches before abandoning him to his own devices.

The Vicar's family-pew was a square stronghold, with high oak walls, which defended its occupants from vulgar observation. As the door closed, the two boys went to their hassocks, sank upon their knees, and buried their faces in their hands. Lady Betty sat for a moment looking at them with adoring love in her heart. They were rude and tiresome in their daily lives, they had no respect for their father, they fought in private, they stole the sugar on those rare occasions when it was unguarded by lock and key, they ate of the fruit which was all forbidden in their mother's orchard, but their faults found expiation in Lady Betty's eyes by this simple act of devotion.

Could she offer to heaven a prayer so innocent and acceptable as theirs? As she knelt she implored with her whole heart to be made trusting and simple as these little children.

The rustling of her dress and the silence that followed were understood by the two boys, and first Samuel, with his mouth open, turned his head cautiously, and then Luke, with his tongue hanging out, did the same, and both perceiving that "teacher" was deep in prayer, they grinned at each other. Then Samuel rummaged in his pocket for a stump of lead pencil, while Luke turned back the cushion silently, after that they began a silent but exciting game of noughts and crosses, which was not without significance.

The bell pealed and then tolled, pews opened and shut, coughing began in good earnest, the clerk took his place in the box under the pulpit, and suddenly Luke turned back the cushion, Samuel concealed the stump of pencil in his capacious mouth, and both buried their faces again, for among the many sounds they distinguished the approaching footsteps of their mother. She looked round at her children and her governess with a feeling of devout satisfaction, and as she also knelt, she considered that it would be false humility to deny that she had done her duty to Heaven and to her family. Then the Reverend John Baxter ascended his pulpit, from which, as from a donjon, he could securely look down into the family fortress below, and the service began.

When the congregation rose, Lady Betty obtained a glimpse of the gallery; she turned her eyes towards the seat occupied by Doctor Blandly, and saw Gerard standing by his side. Her face flushed with pleasure, and a sign of recognition passed between them which did not escape Mrs. Baxter. Who could this thin, elegant young gentleman be? she asked herself, a friend of Doctor Blandly's? Why had she heard nothing of him from Baxter? Was he engaged to Lady Betty? if so, why had she not discovered the fact under that delicate cross-examination to which she had been subjected during the week? When they met at the church-door after the service, she learnt that his name was Gerard Talbot, and it somewhat reconciled her to her husband's departure to think that she should know all that was to be known of the stranger when Baxter returned at night.

As soon as Lady Betty was alone with Gerard, Doctor Blandly leading the way with Baxter across the meadow from the Vicarage, she said, taking his arm:

"Thank you, Gerard."

"For what, Lady Betty?"

"For coming so early."

"Didn't you expect me?"

"Not so early. The first coach does not arrive on Sunday before half-past eleven; I asked."

"Then you hoped I might come early!"

"Of course I did! It must cost a great deal for a carriage all that distance from London."

"It cost me nothing, I walked."

"Oh, poor Gerard! You must be worn out."

Gerard laughed.

"'Tis no distance for a man," said he. "Such a morning as this would tempt me to walk, if I were ten times lazier."

"'Twas not the morning that induced you to come; if it had rained ever so hard you would have come all the same. You said to yourself, 'it will please my sister to see me in church,' and that was sufficient."

" Perhaps it would have been sufficient had I said to myself, 'it will please me to see my sister.'"

"You use the very words that Tom would have used, Gerard," sighed she.

He did not reply, and she, attributing the shade of sadness which had overcast his face to recollections of his dead brother, endeavoured to remove the effect her words had produced by changing the subject.

" Have you written much of your comedy this week ?" she asked.

"I have finished the first act. Last night I saw Mr. Kemble, and he promises to read what I have done, and give me his opinion, if I take it to him next week."

" Oh, that is famous news. You must have worked very hard."

" I found it easier to write thinking of

all you said last Sunday. You have given me hope and courage."

" 'Tis little enough I can do to help you, Gerard. I am not clever, and 'tis not with cleverness I would help you, for I would have the glory of succeeding to be due to you alone. But all that I can do to make your task less difficult, your life less burdensome, that I will do with all my heart." She paused, and they were both silent for a time, then she continued: "I have been trying to think in these last few moments how I can be of service to you, but I can find no means of gratifying my wish. I am like a poor bankrupt who sees distress all around him, and has no means of giving relief. What can I do?"

Gerard's arm trembled beneath her hand as he said in a low voice:

"Suffer me to hope."

"For success, Gerard? why that is

assured. I am certain that your comedy will be well accepted."

"I have built hopes far higher than the mere triumph of my brain. Knowing what I have been, what I am, I dare scarcely tell myself all that my soul desires."

"Whisper but a word, and I will guess the rest. Why should you conceal anything from me? Is there anyone living dearer to me than you?"

"If you knew how solitary my life has been, how utterly alone and uncared for I have stood amongst my fellow-creatures, you would understand the emotion that your mere friendship produces, and readily perceive what hope my exalted imagination conceives."

Lady Betty looked at the agitated man beside her in perplexity a moment, and then:

"Is it my affection you hope for?" she asked.

"It is indeed."

"Why, Gerard, you have it. Are you not my brother as well as his? How doubtful you men are. Tom, my husband, doubted of my love, and you, my brother, of my affection. Kiss me, Gerard—kiss my lips, and doubt no more that I am in truth your sister."

Gerard bent and touched her willing lips, and she looked at him afterwards with wide eyes, her cheeks pale with anxiety for his peace, and finding him still troubled, she did what a woman usually does in such emergencies, turned the subject, and endeavoured to interest him in indifferent matters.

"What a fool my passion has made me—how blind and rash," thought Gerard; "but that her thoughts of love can dwell only on poor Tom, she would have caught the meaning of my words, and straightway I must have lost her affection and respect together."

The Reverend John Baxter sat down to his dinner in the merriest of moods; he grew grave after the roast, and learned with the pie; after that he loosened the lower button of his waistcoat, and attacked the port in silence. Lady Betty led the way with Gerard to the garden; the doctor and the parson were so long to follow, that it was to be presumed they took that which is the best digestive of a good dinner—a doze. However, they were both wide awake when they at length made their appearance, and neither Gerard nor Lady Betty showed any signs of impatience.

"Jerry will bring us a dish of tea to settle our spirits, and then, Gerard, we will hear the new comedy," said Doctor Blandly.

A table was set under the apple-tree,

and when Jerry had served the tea, Doctor Blandly placed a chair before the board for Lady Betty, and was about to seat himself, when he stopped abruptly, and turning to Jerry, said with asperity—

"How is this, Sir? Only three chairs for four people. Fetch another, instantly."

Gerard, as the younger, stood; the two elder gentlemen seated themselves. Presently Jerry returned carrying a velvet-covered chair.

"'Tis Tom's!" cried Lady Betty, catching sight of it, and half-rising from her seat, alarmed less the sacred seat should be profaned.

"Then I think, my dear, it will be very proper that we ask Gerard to use it," said Doctor Blandly, with quiet firmness.

Lady Betty smiled faintly, and murmured: "He is next in our hearts."

And so Gerard took Tom's place in the

empty chair, as Doctor Blandly had doubtless intended he should. Before the cups were empty, Dr. Blandly, with Lady Betty's permission, lit his pipe, that he might, with the philosophic calm produced by the smoke of good birdseye, consider the merits of the literary work about to be read; and then looking round to see that the Reverend John Baxter was also in full possession of his faculties, he said:

"Now, Sir; for the comedy."

And Gerard, without hesitation, opened his manuscript and read.

A very good picture they formed, that little company sitting under the appletree, against a background of peaches and pink hollyhocks. Lady Betty in her black crape dress with short sleeves, her long white, round arms resting upon her lap; Doctor Blandly, with his shapely legs crossed, his portly person, his fair, strong, yet kindly face, his head thrown well back in critical expectancy, and pouting his lips over the waxed end of his long pipe; the Reverend John Baxter with his elbow on his knee, his chin upon his thumb, his index finger sagely pointed towards his red nose, his brows knitted with intense intellectual application; and lastly, Gerard, spare, white and anxious, seated in his brother's chair, and turned with his face towards Lady Betty, holding the manuscript before him.

CHAPTER X.

BARNABAS AND HIS COURT.

WHILE the wines in the cellar of Talbot House held out, Barnabas realised his own ideal of happiness. He lived royally, according to his own conception. His court was composed of the half-dozen rascals who had supported his entrance to the estate, and the vagabond lawyer served for prime minister. His leg was yet painful; he could not move about without a stick or some such support, but this inconvenience was of small importance, as he had no inclination for exercise, and rarely stirred from his seat. He sat at the head of the long oak table, in the grand old banqueting-hall in a capacious high-backed chair, his leg supported on cushions, one hand resting on a Venetian glass, and the other holding a halfpenny clay pipe. His lawyer sat at his right hand, his followers sat below, each man with a bottle and a paper of tobacco before him.

He boasted and lied, and his court listened. He told old filthy jests, and they roared with laughter; he swore, and they looked grave. If anyone fell asleep under the influence of the drink before him, he rose from his seat, *maugre* his leg, took a candle from the sconce, and set fire to the sleeper's hair, or poured red wine down his neck, and limped back to his seat grinning malignantly. He was too vile to laugh heartily, even at the success of his own practical jokes. When he himself was besotted and drowsy, he swept bottles and glasses off the table, sprawled out his arms, and laid his leaden head upon them moaning and grunting until his drunkenness had passed off, and he could sit up to drink again. They never went to bed, never changed their linen, never touched water, but sat there, drinking and sleeping, occasionally eating, perpetually smoking, until the floor was strewn with broken bottles and gnawed bones, and the great room stunk with the filthy tobacco, and the reek of that foul company. One day Barnabas awaking from a long sleep, more sober than usual, looked round upon the litter of broken bottles and his sleeping comrades, and after five minutes cogitation, roared out for Slink.

"How many bottles are there in the cellar?" he asked, when Slink appeared at the door.

"About a score, your honour."

"What!" shouted Barnabas.

Slink repeated his answer, keeping on the alert to dodge the bottle which Barnabas generally hurled when displeased.

"Come here, and help me up. I'll go and see for myself."

He hobbled down to the cellar with much difficulty and profuse blasphemy, and ascertained that Slink had told him nothing but the truth. Then swearing at his friends, at himself for his insane liberality, he locked the cellar-door, and returned to his customary seat with the key in his pocket. From that moment he did not part with it except when he wanted a bottle for his own consumption.

When his fellows awoke and called for refreshment, Barnabas bade Slink bring a can of water, and bluntly told them that they would get no other kind of liquor at his expense in future. The moment that this new regulation was found to be no practical joke but a serious fact, the company withdrew to the other end of the table and held a council, while Barnabas smoked and looked at them in sullen indifference. At the end of a brief conference, the lawyer came forward as spokesman and addressed Barnabas.

"Your friends have got business to do. They wish to be paid for their services and to go to their homes," said he.

"Well, pay them, and let them go," replied Barnabas, with an oath.

"I have no money."

"You said the steward had the collecting of the rents."

"He refuses to give me anything."

"And quite right too—send for him."

The steward was sent for and presently came.

"You have had some rents to collect from the cottages: where is it?" asked Barnabas.

"In my keeping," replied Blake.

"Give it to me."

"Not a penny-piece," said Blake, folding his arms. "My orders be to give all that comes in to Doctor Blandly."

"What has Doctor Blandly to do with my estate?"

"Doctor Blandly is Mr. Tummus's agent, and I'm his servant."

"Well, then you can just go and serve Mr. Thomas," Barnabas said with a sneer and another oath; "and if you are not off the estate in half an hour, I'll have you kicked off."

"The first man that lays his hand on me shall be taken to the lock-up, and the rest after them, if they dare to interfere with me."

"We will soon see about that! Take

the old fool and pitch him into the horsepond, you fellows."

No one moved a hand. He swore and threatened in vain. The steward stood unmoved.

"You and that old idiot the Doctor, shall answer for this," cried Barnabas, smashing a glass down on the floor. "Do you still refuse to obey me?"

"Yes. I serve only Doctor Blandly, and these are my orders. You are to be suffered to remain at the Hall and keep what company and servants you like at your own expense. You are to be allowed to shoot game for your own use. But if you offer a single bird for sale, or remove but one article from the house, or cut so much as a single branch from one of the trees, I'm to take the lawyer's papers before the nearest magistrate and demand his protection of Mr. Thomas's property."

"The property's mine now my brother is dead."

"Ah! you'll have to prove that."

Barnabas turned to his lawyer, who appeared to be not at all surprised at what he heard.

"Here, what's to be done?" he asked.

The lawyer shrugged his shoulders.

"Do you want to know anything more of me?" asked the steward.

"Get out, curse you!" shouted Barnabas.

Humphrey Blake left the room.

"You said I could take possession," said Barnabas.

"You have," replied his counsellor.

"But how am I to defeat this cursed Doctor Blandly?"

"Find the body of your brother, and you can laugh at him."

"By George, I will. Set a score of fellows to drag the river from end to end."

"Give me the money to pay them."

"I haven't a guinea. Raise money for me—I'll sign any paper you like—you shall make your own terms for payment when I get the money."

"It is impossible to raise money until your title is established."

"You said you could make a case for the Chancery Courts."

"So I can, but not without money. You owe me a long bill now."

"But I'll pay you what you ask when I get my title—why don't that satisfy you?"

"Because I don't believe you ever will get your title."

Amidst the storm of oaths and imprecations that followed this announcement, the lawyer and his associates withdrew, merely putting in their pockets such articles of value as they could conceal from the vigilant eyes of the steward, and one by one sneaked away from the Hall and its penniless tenant, with no intention of returning.

The only immediate regret Barnabas felt in their departure was, that it had not taken place before. They had drunk best part of his wine, and what should he do when he had finished the remainder? The question was fraught with such gloomy forebodings that he despatched it from his thoughts, determining to face the evil when it came—as often before he had shirked the reflection that he would be hanged at some subsequent date. It was when night came, and the candles failed to light up the further corners of the large room, that he missed his companions. The dim corners had a fascination for his eyes, which grew with the terrible pictures that came before his heated and disordered imagination. He pictured Tom in the likeness of a corpse he had once seen drawn from a pond after long lying there, and fancied him stepping in that hideous mortality from out the gloom.

"Light all the candles!" he said to Slink.

"There be but a dozen left, master, and they are nigh down to the sockets," said Slink, as he moved to obey the command.

He asked himself what night would be with neither companions, nor wine, nor light. The reflection was productive of a fresh command:

"Fetch me another bottle, and then blow out every candle but one."

As the lights one after the other were blown out he drank the bottle, his eyes wandering from corner to corner; when only one was left he shut his eyes and tried to sleep.

The next day he sent Slink out to sell his horse. Slink obeyed with a sorry heart, for the horse had been his comfort through the miserable months, and had improved in appearance under his careful grooming, since the first unlucky day it was given to him. He had not the spirit to higgle over the sale, and accepting the first offer that was made for the beast, he brought his master forty shillings, and had a bottle flung at his head for his pains. The money was spent in candles and strong ale.

Once more at night-time he forced Slink to play at picquet, but with nothing to gain and no inducement to cheat, the play had so little hold upon his mind, that his senses were for ever wandering to catch strange noises or the fantastic shadows thrown by a guttering candle. His only recourse was to stupify his brain with tobacco and beer.

One moring he limped up the staircase and along the great corridor to examine the chambers. They were all large, but one seemed less awful than the rest, and he decided upon going there at night, thinking to sleep sounder in a bed than cramped over a table. But when the light faded, he dared not go away from the banqueting-hall—that at least he knew; its nooks and hollows were familiar to him.

The corridor was mysterious even in the light which came through the coloured oriel window at the end, it would be awful at night. And the chamber —might it not have a secret door; might he not find something lying in the bed when he opened it; these reflections passed through his muddled, enfeebled, guilty mind, and kept him to the larger room.

There was no one in the great house but himself and Slink. Slink was indispensable. He shot the game, cooked it, ate with him, submitted to his bullying, slept in the same room lying on the sofa, in that dark corner which Barnabas feared most, and waited on him with the docility and patience of a born servant. But he added not a little to his nightly terrors.

When he detected his master pausing to listen, in the act of raising a glass to his lips, he showed the liveliest symptoms of dread, ejaculating, "Oh, Lord!" and "merciful powers defend us!" and fell a chattering with his teeth as though in an ague; if Barnabas dropped his pipe, and fixed his eyes upon the obscurity, Slink would drop on his knees, imploring the angels to have mercy upon him.

"What are you afeard of?" Barnabas asked one night. "You've fastened the shutters and barred all the doors, haven't you?"

"All the doors I knows on, master; but what does that signify! The place is like a rabbit warren; there's a dozen passages only known to the rightful owners; a dozen doors as open secret-like into the west wing. You can smell the mouldering walls and the rotten floors when you pass by the big staircase, for all its bein' shut off this hund'ed years, and closed with boards and green baize that the great, long-legged spiders and woodlouses crawl over. What's doors to ghostes?"

"Ghosts! What are you talking about? D'ye think I take heed of such rubbish?"

"It may be rubbish, but I've heard as murdered men must walk till they're laid with bell and candle, and whose to lay Master Tom, when his body's —— Oh, good Lord! what are you looking at, master?"

"Hold your cursed tongue, and go sit over yonder where the curtain hangs."

CHAPTER XI.

THE MEETING OF OLD FRIENDS.

IT was a wretched existence that Slink led even in the broad light of day, when Barnabas himself was free from superstitious apprehensions.

Humphrey Blake, having sifted all the evidence he could collect, had arrived at a tolerably close approximation to the truth. Why Doctor Blandly pooh-poohed his conclusions he did not know; he was equally in the dark as to the true relationship of Barnabas to the Talbot family.

What he maintained, with the persevering obstinacy of conceit, was that Barnabas was an imposter, and in all probability Master Tom's murderer. Doctor Blandly's obstinacy in refusing to credit his belief piqued the egotistical old man's pride, and strengthened his desire to prove the truth of his convictions. One person could if he chose reveal the fact, and he was Slink.

But Slink, for a very good reason, was silent and stubborn, and refused not only to tell the latter events in his master's career, but to reveal any of his antecedents, despite the most artful and persevering cross-examination to which the steward subjected him. Wrath against him for his contumacy rather than for any supposed participation in the murder, Blake unwisely removed the one chance he had of making discoveries—he forbade Jenny, on pain of being sent away to her maiden aunt in Lancashire, to speak to Slink. On the other hand, he threatened Slink with the most severe punishment if he caught him sneaking about the lodge.

By these means he hoped to bring the lad to confess; but as time went on and Slink made no sign of submission, he extended his punishment by forbidding the workers on the estate to have any communication with Slink, so that the poor fellow suffered all the pains of ostracism, with the additional pain of knowing those who shunned him for old friends. Master Blake refused to let him have even the company of a dog, and forbade him to enter any of the stables except that set apart for his master's horse. There would have been pleasure in shooting hares with a dog to start them from their coverts; there was none in hunting alone.

One morning he shot a woodpigeon,

and as he was jumping down the bank into the road, to secure the fluttering bird, his ears were greeted with the sound of a well-remembered voice, crying in a rich brogue:

" Well done, me boy; I couldn't a hit um better myself."

Turning round he discovered the old pedlar, Barney O'Crewe, seated on the bank, with his pack on one side of him, a bottle on the other, and three inches of black clay pipe between his fingers.

" Whoy faix, 'tis my own swate friend, Toby!" the pedlar exclaimed, rising and then grasping Slink's hand, he added: " Oi'm charmed to renew th' acquaintince, darlint."

The devil himself, with such a warm demonstration of friendship, would have been welcome to the unhappy Slink; whatever doubts he might have had as to the pedlar's sincerity were forgotten, and hearing the unctious voice, he could only remember the songs and stories which had delighted him in the loft on the night of their previous meeting. He grinned from ear to ear, and beamed grateful acknowledgemet of the friendly overtures.

"An' y'are out in the mornun a shootin' birds and bastes, like a rale gentleman, as y'are."

Slink nodded assent.

"It does me good to see the same," continued the pedlar. "And is the master wid yer?"

"He's at the Hall, being laid up with a broken leg, but it's nigh healed now."

"Ah! he's got into the Hall, has he? good luck to him; and he's taken his own proper name, Mr. Thaophilus Talbot, Esquoire?"

Slink nodded again.

"Well, my boy, ye shall jist take me

up to the Hall the way ye've come, for I'm not proud, and I've a moighty pradelection against passing the lodge, which is the raison I've been resting myself on this sod for the last hour, takun a philosophicle look at things. Putt your lips, to commence wid, at the bottle, darlint; you know the flavor of it, ye divil, ye deu! Putt the bird in your pockut, 'tis an illigant bird, to be sure, and a murtherin' sin to lave it behint."

Slink pocketed the bird, and with a glance down the road to be sure that Master Blake was not in sight, assisted the old pedlar in climbing up the bank and entering the wood. When these difficulties were overcome, the garrulous Barney recommenced talking, leaning affectionately upon the arm of his young friend.

"I've been a prayun to the blessed

saints for ye, darlint, and I hope to goodness the master trates ye koindly."

"That's all right," said Slink.

"Beca'se 'tis a jewel in his crown to have a faithful sarvint, and there's few in the warld that's the loikes of you, divil a wan! ye desarve to be trated handsome, and ye shall be, for oim goun to stay a bit wid the master, and I'll spake a good word in your favor, besides entertainin' ye wid all the beautiful songs and stories in my rickollection, wid a taste of the bottle in betwixt and betwane."

Slink's face expanded in the broadest of grins.

"Ye shall take another taste of the same, immagiate as a token, darlint."

He stopped, drew out the stone bottle from his pack, and having administered the dose and resumed his march, he said, in a tone more wheedling and soft than ever:

"'Tis the blessed saints as guided ye to me this mornun in answer to my prayers, for I've been a dyun to see you a long toime, and have an agraible convirsation wid ye. And now ye shall tell me all what's been a happenin' to ye since I bade ye good-bye at the 'Lone Crow.'"

He paused to give Slink an opportunity of acting upon his suggestion, but finding him disinclined to break silence he continued:

"I've been making inquoiries in the town, and the inn beyond the hill, and they tell me that Misther Thomas Talbot has been croally murthered, but I can't belave it; is it thrue, now?"

Slink nodded.

"Why wasn't I borned a lawyer?" Barney asked himself, and then with a smile he said: "So you know he was murthered. Now can you tell me in sacret and confidance who murthered 'um?"

"No, I can't," said Slink, stoutly.

"Well, that bothers me complately, for they tells me it was the master as murthered 'um, and seein' you follows 'um loike his own blessed shadder, 'tis impossable he could have done it and you not know. So I say, darlint, that y'are mistuk. Master Thomas was not murthered."

"Yes he was."

"But I say he was nut; and so how can ye say he was?"

"Because he was shot and——" Slink stopped suddenly.

"And buried dacent in the river. Thrue for you, my swate friend; but how d'ye know he was shot, seein' his body was niver brought to light?"

Slink bent his brows in silence.

"I'd a been a raal judge, and done

nothun but putt on the black cap from mornun' til night, if Providence had edicated me to the laigal profission," thought the pedlar.

"Look here, Sir," said Slink, "you'll see the master directly, and he can tell you all you want to know, I daresay. Let's talk about something else."

The amiable pedlar was so well pleased with himself and Slink that he made no objection to this proposal, but entered at once upon the narration of several anecdotes, which made the road to the Hall too short to his admiring companion.

Barnabas was no less pleased than Slink had been to see the pedlar. He had need of a lively companion, and hoped that his father's superior cunning would enable him in a short time to be independant of assistance. He concealed his feelings, however, as well as he could, and only responded to O'Crewe's flattery and protestations of " ondying affliction" with a grunt or a nod.

Nothing daunted by this cold reception, the pedlar exerted himself to amuse his son, and get him into a good temper, and so far succeeded in raising him from his morbid prostration, that he saw the candles lit without a shudder, and bade Slink get out of the room directly after, partly because he could do without him, but chiefly because Slink evidently enjoyed the pedlar's conversation, and wished to stay.

Banished from the room, Slink contented himself with listening at the keyhole to the pedlar's songs and stories, until clapping his eye to the key-hole, after a minute's silence, he perceived him walking towards the door, when he retired with alacrity, and took refuge in a deep embrasure by the great stairs. From this hiding-place he saw the door open, and the pedlar come out and stand in a listening attitude for a moment or two, then return to the room, closing the door after him.

It was some time before he dared return to the door, but at length the misery of sitting alone in the dark and silence while good things were being said in the adjacent room overcame his fears of discovery, and he cautiously approached the convenient key-hole, and bent his ear to listen.

" 'Tis moighty hard, and so it is, to get the hold truth out of ye, Barney, my darlint," the pedlar was saying. "It does ye credit, and I'm proud on ye. If you was as simple as your sarvint, Slink, I'd turn ye inside out like a pair o' leather breeches in half a minit. If ye knowed how I've been a prayun to the holy saints, and sthrugglin' and sthrivin' to learn the blessed truth, to help ye in your misfortunes, ye'd be more agraible and complaisaint. Isn't it all for your own good, my blessed Barney, that I'd have you revale the holy sacrets of your bussom to me? Sure, I larned more from that swate innocint lamb, Mr. Slink, in two minutes than ye've condescended to tell me in half-an-hour."

"What has he told you—blabbing hound!"

"Nothing at all but to your honour. He only towld me how you shot um and throwed his body in the wather."

"It's a lie."

"To be sure, I made a mistake. 'Twas you shot 'im, and the lad that throwed um into the river."

"I'll stop the fool's tongue; I'll have his life to-morrow."

"Barney, my darlint, y'are right. You

shall have his life—but not to-morrow, my brave boy."

"What do you mean?"

"Listen to me, swaitest. Ye want ividence of Masther Tom's death in order that ye may come into your holy rights and trew inheritince, don't ye?"

"Well?"

"Supposun to-morrow mornun, soon as the glorious sun is a-spreadun a blush of beauty over the charmun face o' nature, I go to the nairest magistrate and says, 'Yer honour, there's a secret on my moind that I must revale or my conscience will droive me to dispiration. I know who 'twas that murthered and did for that gentleman of quality, Mr. Thomas Talbot?'"

"Will you betray me?"

"Not a bit of it, darlint. Putt down the bottle when you've took a drink. This is how the whole business wull be transacted. I'll say to the magistrate, 'If it plase your honour, Sor, I was walkun' along quite paceable by the side of the river, thinkin' o' nothing in the world but the blessed saints in heaven, whan I see a man on horseback comun' towards me, and takun' um to be no better than a highwayman, I jumped t'other side the hedge, and laid there wid my pack in mortal tripidation and almoighty fear, till of a suddint I heard a pistol-shot and a scrame, and the nixt moment I seed a horse run bye widout no one on his back at all at all, and the blessed Virgin inspirin' me wid the courage of a lion I crept along behint the hedge so as I couldn't be seen till I come in sight of a blackguard as was draggun' a gintleman into the cowld water. By the light of the blessed moon ——' "

" There wasn't a moon."

" Thankye for the hint, my charmer.

'By the loight of the swate stars I see the countenance of the gintleman and the face of the blackguard perfectly clair. The face of the blackguard I shall niver forget to me dyun day. It terrified me to sich a degree that I took to my heels to save myself.' Whan I've told the magistrate this I shall woipe the prespiration off my brow, and I shall continy : ' Well, Sor, goun wid my pack to Talbot Hall to see if I could sell the gentry a paper of pins, or a small-comb, who should I foind there, in the livery of a sarvant, but the very blackguard I see a murthering the gintleman by the river, and it's him I'd have you take into custody.' What do you think o' that, Barney darlint ?"

"What am I to say, for they'll come questioning me, plague take 'em."

" Nothun at all, darlint. Divil a word.

Ye'll just take your oath that you don't know nothun about ut, but that sure enough ye gave Slink lave to go and see his swateheart, and he didn't come back to ye till the mornun, wid a cock-and-bull story of gettun drunk over night; and since then, ye'll add, the varmunt has been playun ducks and drakes wid the money like water, gettun dronk, and flirtun wid the wenches."

"And then Slink will tell his story. How then?"

"Let um. Wait till I get in the witness-box. I know how to manage um. I'll terrify um wid my eye. I'll make the varmint swear black's white, and thremble and stutter and make such a fool of a liar of himself that the intilligent jury will be bound to hang um. I'll get the compliments and flattery of the judge and all the illigant lawyers for me ability, trust me."

"And what good will all this do me?"

"What good, d'ye ax? Faix, and 'tis not my own son that will ax the question twoice. Sure, whan they've hanged Slink for murtherin' your brother, they can't dispute that the murthered man's dead; and then what's to bar your inhiritance? And we will hang un as sure as justice."

Slink waited to hear no more.

About ten o'clock Barnabas roared for him—having emptied the great pot of ale. He roared a second time, and there was no answer.

Then the pedlar went to the door, and called out in his blandest tones:

"Toby, darlint, whoy don't ye come when yer master calls? Where are you, swaitest?"

But his seductive appeal failed to elicit

response from Slink, and for a very good reason: he was ten miles from Sevenoaks on his road to London.

CHAPTER XII.

FLIGHT AND PURSUIT.

SLINK made his way to London through Ightham, Wrotham and Gravesend, feeling himself safer on the road he knew. He had not a farthing in his pocket, and in the morning hunger became unendurable. A stable-keeper gave him sixpence and as much as he wanted to eat and drink for a day's work in his stable. At night he continued his journey, but the rain falling heavily compelled him to take refuge in a barn, where he slept until the morning.

About midday Saturday he arrived at Edmonton, and rang the bell at Doctor Blandly's. Old Kate came to the gate, and bade him call in the evening; her master and Jerry had gone a-fishing. She could not say where they were, and advised him to go wait in the "Bell."

This was capital advice to a man with money, but Slink had spent his sixpence on the road, and was once more hungry and penniless. He dared not sit on the settle outside the inn, for he doubted not but that the pedlar had sworn information against him, and that all the country was in pursuit of him.

He turned up the little lane beside the Doctor's garden, and lay in a meadow until the sun went down, then he carefully approached the main road, and again rang at the Doctor's bell. This time Jerry came in response.

"Master's dining, but you can come in. If your business ben't very important, you had better wait till he's finished."

"Oh, my business ben't important. It's only a matter of life and death, and as I've waited since the morning, there's no reason why I shouldn't wait another hour or so—albeit I've had nothing betwixt my teeth since ten o'clock."

"Oh, you're one of those 'tis-but-tisn't, might-be-but can't, gentry, I see. You'd better follow me, case I get blamed for your fault."

Slink followed Jerry, and having duly scraped his feet, and rubbed them well heels and side on a mat, he took off his hat, smoothed down his hair, and entered the dining-room when Jerry was satisfied with his presentability.

"Well, my man; what have you got to

say to me?" the Doctor asked, with his mouth full.

Slink twisted his hat round, and glanced from the Doctor to Jerry, and back again to the Doctor without replying.

"Don't you hear what's said to you?" asked Jerry.

"Yes, Sir; but if you please, I don't want to speak before you, Sir."

The Doctor laughed heartily. "Well, you won't mind his knowing where you come from, I daresay," said he.

"Sevenoaks, your honour."

"Jerry, take that young fellow down to the kitchen, and give him a mug of ale and a thumb-piece; he hasn't anything in his stomach, I know by the sound of his voice. And don't worry him, do you hear, Jerry? When you're a bit refreshed, return to me here, my lad."

Slink obeyed with alacrity, and reappeared in the dining-room surprisingly soon, considering the quantity of ale and bread and cheese he had consumed in the interval; but he had a wide mouth and a large throat, and his excellent digestive organs were equal to any task imposed upon them.

"Now, my lad, what is it?" the Doctor asked, clearing a space in front of him to rest his arms upon, as Jerry withdrew and closed the door. "Have you come from Mr. Blake, the steward?"

"Not exactly, your honour, but very near, as one may say. It was the steward's daughter as told me to come to you."

"His daughter—the wench with red cheeks?"

"And beautiful dark eyes, your honour," Slink sighed.

"Ha! ha! The same story everywhere," the Doctor said half to himself.

"Well, well; and why has she sent you to me?"

"Because she said you would stand by me if I told you the whole truth, and wouldn't let them hang me."

"Great Heavens!—hang you!—what for?"

"For murdering Master Tom."

Doctor Blandly raised himself in his chair, and looked at Slink in blank astonishment for a minute, then said in an altered tone:

"If this deed is yours alone, tell me nothing. I am loath to be instrumental to the death even of a criminal, unless it is absolutely my duty. If then you killed this poor gentleman of your own will and purpose, say not a word to me, but go out by that door while I close my eyes. But if—as by your appearance it seems to me more likely—you have been but the tool in the hands of a more villainous man, tell me what is on your mind, and I will do what I may to befriend you."

"God bless your honour! the guilt is not on my head. Let me tell you just what happened the night afore last as I listened at the door in Talbot Hall." And then Slink related the conversation he had overheard between Barnabas and his father; in conclusion he said: "When I heard their scheme to bring me to the gallows, then I made up my mind to run away into the woods and hide myself there; but I couldn't go without first saying good-bye to my sweetheart, and begging her to disbelieve the wicked things they said against me, and it was she as bade me come to you and confess everything, 'For,' says she 'the Doctor's the justest man that ever lived, and won't see you hung for your master's crime,' she says."

The Doctor spoke, but Slink heard

nothing but the sound of the bell which was at that moment pulled. Looking through the window, he saw over the tops of the gate, the eye and wrinkled forehead, and grey hair of Barney O'Crewe.

"My God!" he cried, "'tis the pedlar! Hide me, Doctor—hide me!"

"One word—is his story true?—did you kill Mr. Talbot?"

"No; I swear to Heaven I didn't."

"Then all the pedlars in the world shan't touch you. Go upstairs, and in the first room you come to, lock the door, and crawl under the bed if you like. Jerry, bring the man at the gate in here if he wants to see me, and say not a word more than is necessary to him on the way."

Slink followed the Doctor's advice to the letter, while Jerry admitted the pedlar and conducted him into Doctor Blandly's presence without returning a single word to his bland inquiries, and persuasive addresses.

"'Tis Docthur Blandly I have the honour of salutin'," said the pedlar.

"That's my name. You can leave the room, Jerry. Return when I ring the bell."

"'Tis a jewel of a servint y'have, Doctor Blandly—a swate, civil spoken old man, as ever drawed the blessed breath of loife, with a dacent habit of holdin' his tongue, which leaves nothun to find fault wid in his speech."

"And who may you be, Sir?"

"The question's a very proper one, and does you credit, Docthor, and I'll answer ye widout any risarvation. I'm Mr. Barnabas O'Crewe."

"Barnabas O'Crewe—the father of the man who calls himself Theophilus Talbot?"

"That's as hereafther may be; at

present you may take it that I'm his perticlar friend. In the first place, Doctor, y'are doubtless aware that the murtherer of Mr. Thomas Talbot, is discivered and brought to loight."

"Who is the murderer?"

"Toby Slink by name—the varmint as stole Mr. Thomas's horse, shot his dog, and finilly slaughtered the young gintleman and throwd him into the cowld river. I see 'um do it wid my own eyes."

"Have you informed the magistrates?"

"I have. I've took my Bible oath on it; and the b'y's as good as hanged. Albeit, he's given us the slip—bad luck to um, and can't be found nowheres. However, oi'll foind um, lave me alone for that, I'll onairth um loike a fish from the blessed ocean. Now, Docthor, we'll preshume that he's hanged, and drawed and quarthered, and all complete, amen! and there's no furder obstacle to Thaophilus

Talbot coming into possession of the funds y'are so kindly taken care of for um."

"Not a farthing, I will throw the estate into Chancery."

"I beg to differ wid ye, Doctor, on a 'pint of law. If the b'y's hung for havin' murthered Mr. Thomas, how will ye proove that the gintleman is aloive?"

"You're a cunning rascal!" cried Doctor Blandly, striking the table with his fist.

"Thank you koindly for the complimint. I trost I'm a bit cliver in the law. Now Thaophilus has promused that I shall live like a prince when he comes into his fortun—he's wullin to make splendid terms wid me to howld my tongue and live in his company."

"Then why don't you hold your tongue?"

"Becase I set no value on all these

riches, for two or three reasons. In the fust place, I don't think I should get 'em; in the second, I want money at oncet to hunt up that varmint Slink, for the public officers won't do their duty widout, bad luck to 'em; and in the third place, I don't hanker after livun in the society of Thaophilus—he's conthracted an onpleasant habut of wakun up in the middle o' the noight and seeun ghostes that makes my blood run cold and oncomfortable."

"Well, well—come to the point."

"Bedad I'm comun to it straght. Docther dear, y' have a koind o' spite against Thaophilus."

"I have the same feeling towards other villains."

"Quoite roight for you, Docther. I know that ye'd much rather see Mr. Gerard in Talbot Hall than his half-brother—for I'll tell you candid and thrue, Doctor, there being no witnesses present, that Mr. Gerard is no son of mine. And now widout no more bating about the bush, if you'll promuse me faithful to give me a thrifle—say two or three hunderd pounds a year for the whole of my life till I die—I'll proove that Mr. Thaophilus is an imposter."

"You will say that of your own son?"

"To be sure will I. For I don't like the principals of um. That gettin up o' nights ain't natr'al and it ain't pleasant, and he'd chate his own father if he had the chance, bad luck to um. I'll swear he was three months old before ever he was registered, and that Admiral Talbot, Heaven rest his sowl—was no more the b'y's father than you are."

With knitted brows Doctor Blandly looked at Barney O'Crewe in silence whilst he considered his proposal. Had he his own inclinations alone to follow, he would have rung the bell for Jerry to show the old vagabond the garden-gate at once, but Gerard was to be thought of, and it was for Gerard to decide whether the evidence of a rascal should be bought and paid for. He felt that the advantages were too great to be relinquished hastily for a scruple, which after all, was one of delicacy rather than conscience.

"Well, Docther dear, and what do you think of ut?"

"What I think of it is of small importance. How Mr. Gerard Talbot takes your offer remains to be seen. I shall set the facts before him to-morrow, and on Monday, if you call here at ten o'clock, you shall know whether he accepts or rejects your proposal."

The Doctor rang the bell, Jerry answered immediately, and his presence stopped Barney O'Crewe from saying anything further upon a matter which he had every reason to keep secret. He had a mortal aversion to witnesses.

CHAPTER XIII.

QUICK AND DEAD.

THE pedlar had parted from his son early on Friday morning with the avowed intention of swearing information against Toby Slink, with the nearest magistrate, and returning to his son "immaidjitly."

"Will you come wid me, Barney, darlint?" he asked.

"'Tisn't likely," replied Barnabas.

"Maybe y'are wise, though y'are not sociable, the saints love ye. Kape ye'r spirits up, me charmer; I'll be back wid ye in the twinklin of an oye."

As a matter of fact the old man never went near the magistrate, having resolved in the course of the night to take that somewhat hazardous course if he could not make satisfactory terms with Doctor Blandly. "A pig by the leg's worth a dozen in the bog; for it's all the warld to a chaney orange you won't catch a hair of their backs--the sly varmints," he said to himself, as lighting his pipe he trudged away from Talbot Hall, with his face towards London and his pack on his back.

Barnabas drank, smoke and dozed until mid-day; then feeling hungry he limped away to the kitchen to get the remains of the hare they had been eating for breakfast, and which his father had cleared away, saying he would make the place look a bit "dacent" in case the magistrates came to question Barnabas. There was not a scrap of food in the kitchen, and the pack which the pedlar had likewise removed for "dacency" was not there either. Barnabas extended his search from place to place until his patience was exhausted, then he took to smashing everything breakable that came in his way, until his fury at finding himself cheated and robbed was abated; after that he sat down and tried to form a plan of revenge. His father had hinted at the "Lone Crow" of compromising with Doctor Blandly, and Barnabas had no doubt that he had gone to sell him.

What could he do to frustrate the plans of the subtle old man? Nothing. He felt himself utterly helpless. Not a soul stood by him; even Slink had abandoned him. His pockets were again empty—for his father, though ignorant of the game of piquet, had shown himself an adept at cheating, and fleeced him of the small residum remaining from the forty shillings brought him by the sale of Slink's horse. And he was hungry—villainously hungry. The very fact of not being able to get anything to eat increased his appetite. Drinking and smoking only heightened his imaginary necessity for food. At length, flinging the old jug at the wall, he rose up from his seat resolved to sell his mare. Prudence told him that before long he might have need of her on the road; "Curse the future," he cried, in reply.

He limped to the stable, with his hat wrong side forward over his eyes, and his stick in his hand. The mare had been neglected since Slink gave her a parting feed, and whinnied as he flung the doors back. "Get over," he growled, hitting her on the flank savagely; the mare obeyed whisking her tail and showing the white of her eyes. He determined to leave the saddle for another day, and having untied the halter from the ring on the manger, he gave the rope a jerk to turn the mare. She was unused to such neglect and rough treatment in the stable, and turned with so little care as to bang Barnabas rudely against the side of the stable. Exasperated by this addition to the morning's wrongs, he lifted his stick, and clenching his teeth, brought it down with all his force upon her back. A kick, a bound, and a scuffle, and the mare wrenched the halter out of her master's hand, bolted into the yard, and through the open gate into the wide and open park. She was a speck in the distance when Barnabas next caught sight of her.

"The Devil's against me," he said, throwing himself upon the grass.

He would have taken the saddle in the

town to sell, but for the superstitious belief that the ill-luck of the day, Friday, would attend him there, and that the saddler, as well as the Devil, would be against him. The rain began to fall, but he lay there in dogged indifference until he was wet through, then shivering with cold he shuffled into the Hall, and sat down beside the beer barrel, where he drank and smoked until about four o'clock. The ale did not make him drunk —it did not even stupify him, it simply depressed him and made his head ache.

He was so completely wretched that had there been a hanging rope or other ready means of destroying himself at hand, he would have committed suicide. He left the barrel with a curse, and went out again into the air. The rain was still falling, heavily, persistently; there was no break in the leaden sky. The ground was soft and spongy, the only sound was the splashing of rain-water and the chattering of sparrows under the eaves; the horizon was veiled with misty clouds.

To stay amid such dismal surroundings would make him mad he felt, so he limped away from it, down the broad drive and through the sodden lane to the nearest ale-house, where if he found no one to sympathise with him, he should at least have the excitement of quarrelling with the innkeeper when it came to the question of paying for what he had consumed.

When the time came for closing the inn he was turned out, and driven into the middle of the road with a kick from the indignant innkeeper, who had unwisely supplied him with bread and cheese, drink and tobacco to the value of thirteenpence.

The rain fell still heavily, without intermittance. There was no light.

Now running against a bank, now stumbling into a ditch, now walking forwards without the slightest knowledge of whither his footsteps were leading him, Barnabas by slow steps came to the lodge, which was discovered by the light gleaming through the chinks of the window-shutter. A horrible dread had seized his mind that he should have to enter that Hall and sleep in the dark, for he did not know where the tinder-box was to be found; perhaps his father had stolen that with the other things.

He knocked, and when Jenny replied, he begged her to give him a lantern in the most abject tone he could command. After a few minutes Jenny opened the window and handed him the light.

" I suppose you're afraid to open the

door to me," he growled, when he had the lantern in his hand.

"I'm no more afraid of you than I am of a rat; but the rats and you too are best outside," she answered, closing the shutters again.

With the lantern swinging by his side he hobbled up the drive, never raising his eyes from the ground until he was close by the terrace steps. The terrors of solitude in the home of the man he had murdered were already taking hold of his imagination. He dreaded the awful silence, broken at long intervals by the strange slight sounds which seem inseparable from an old house, and which have no explanation. He dreaded the snatches of sleep that would overpower his senses for awhile, and end with the sudden awakening from a dream so hideous as to defy passive endurance. He dreaded being aroused from forgetfulness by the sputtering of a candle, to find shadows leaping from the floor to the ceiling in the flickering light of a fallen wick.

He paused on the first step to ask himself if it were not wiser to sleep in the empty stable, and then he raised his eyes to the house furtively, and for the first time. There was a light there. Not in the banqueting chamber, but in the room on the other side of the entrance. The lantern rattled as it hung on his quivering finger.

What did the light signify? Had his father and Slink combined, and laid evidence against him, and were the officers of justice come to take him away to gaol? That was the least of his fears; the more terrible were indefinable—a vague, awful apprehension of the unknown conjured up a thousand ghostly figures, grotesque and horrible. But the light was real; it glowed steadily. He could count the bricks in the casement. There was nothing supernatural in the appearance; no figures such as danced before his eyes in the delirium of fear looked out at him, grinning with fleshless chops, beckoning with rotten fingers! And if the dead were not feasting in that house what had he to fear? Not the living. Justice would have followed him to the ale-house and trapped him there, not waited with uncovered light in the Hall for him to run like a fool into an unbaited trap.

"'Tis the pedlar returned," he said to himself, with an effort to convince himself on the point. And why should it not be? Might he not have been detained by the magistrates? That was most probable. Yet it was with trembling steps he ascended to the terrace. He paused to listen; not a sound reached his straining ear. The sot had fallen asleep, he concluded, still he dared not lay his hand upon the door. He stole towards the window; they were too high from the ground for him to see into the lower part of the room. He went back to the door, and raised his hand as if to turn the handle, then dropped it like a thing of lead by his side. He looked around him. Within the radius of light cast by the candle in his lantern he saw the black moss upon the grey stone of the terrace, and the rain dropping vertically; beyond—nothing. Should he call the pedlar? His throat was too dry, and his tongue had lost its office. He must do something—enter the house or fly. Fly—whither could he fly? If the dead was in the house, would it let him sleep or rest. . . . .

He pursed his lips, whistled low, and listened. He fancied he heard a voice. It gave him courage, for he had caught the pedlar speaking aloud to himself the night before. He whistled again and louder. Certainly a voice spoke. The light upon the casement moved slowly. A dark figure came to the window, but from where he stood Barnabas could see nothing but a break in the light. The figure retired; a door creaked. The lantern fell with a clatter upon the stones at his feet; there was a rushing in his ear as if water were closing over his head. The chain upon the door fell, the bolt grated in the lock, an unseen hand opened the great oak door, and raised a candle high, and under the light of it Barnabas saw standing face to face with him, in the very habit that he wore, Tom Talbot!

With a rattling in his parched throat he fell forward, flat upon the wet stone, like a log.

CHAPTER XIV.

PANDORA'S BOX.

WHEN Lady Betty looked from the fortress under the pulpit on the following Sunday morning, she was surprised to see Gerard standing alone in Doctor Blandly's pew. She had seen the Doctor on Saturday morning in perfect health, and was at a loss to account for his absence.

"Why are you alone, Gerard?" she asked, when they met after the service.

"It is by my fault, I fear," he replied. "I was late in leaving town this morning, and believing that Doctor Blandly would go on without me, I came directly to the church, instead of going to him first in the ordinary way. He doubtless has stayed at home waiting for me."

" I was afraid some accident had happened to him, you looked so grave and serious this morning."

" I am not a gay fellow at the best of times," said Gerard.

Lady Betty looked at him with quick suspicion, and asked :

" Are these not the best of times then, Gerard ?"

" I think we must go round by the road; the heavy rains of this past miserable week must have made the meadow impassable."

" Let it be the road," she answered, and they walked on in silence until they were clear of the homeward-wending congregation, she glancing furtively now and again at him, then pressing his arm a little closer to her side, she said: "Tell me what is the matter, Gerard."

"Mr. Kemble has read the first act of my comedy and condemned it."

"Is that all?" cried Lady Betty, with a laugh. "Why, then, be gay. Merit has ever to face the spite of envy."

"But Mr. Kemble is neither envious nor spiteful. 'Twas with pain he gave me his honest criticism to save me from greater disappointment and waste of time."

"Granted he be honest in his opinion, what then? 'Tis but the opinion of one man, as likely to be mistaken as another. Were we not all charmed with your work when you read it to us under the apple-tree? do you think Doctor Blandly would flatter? do you think I am insincere?"

"God forbid! 'Tis because you are

sincere in your friendship that I cannot take your judgment as unbiassed."

"And if 'tis so, why should you be discouraged? Say that the act has less merit than we believe, and more faults than Mr. Kemble, with all his generous amity, can point out, 'tis but the fifth part of your comedy, and your comedy is but a fractional part of that which your brain contains. If we were judged by single efforts, the ablest of mankind might be debased, the feeblest exalted. Do we judge Shakespeare by the first few pages that he wrote?"

"Dear girl, would you have me put on wings, and fly to a height from which the fall must break me?"

"But you have genius to sustain you. You took up the pen, feeling that you could write, and that consciousness should be your assurance."

"I took up the pen by necessity, and

learnt too late that poets are born, not made. I am not a poet; I am—nothing!"

The tone of despondency in which he spoke was stronger than argument; it forced Lady Betty to doubt her own judgment. She was silent for some seconds, then she said:

"Gerard, you told me one Sunday that I gave you strength and courage to persevere; do you remember?"

"Perfectly, and 'tis true. If I have wrote one worthy line, 'twas in a happy moment which you had made hopeful."

"I have not altered, why should my influence fail? Let me inspire you with yet greater hope. 'Tis my dearest wish to help you, to be of womanly service to you, to hold the cup to your lips, and brighten your existence by all the means I have."

Gerard felt his heart stirred, and his

blood running quicker through his veins as he listened to these affectionate words and looked into the girl's sweet earnest face. He thought how admirable she was, how weak he.

" You put me to the blush," he said ; " I am ashamed of my faint heart."

" 'Tis diffidence alone," said she; " your only fault is in setting too high a value on the careless or partial criticism of this Mr. Kemble. And who is he? a player, forsooth! who judges a play by the scope it affords his powers."

" 'Tis not a careless criticism; he pointed out a hundred defects which I perceive are real."

" And I," cried Lady Betty, " will point out a thousand merits which you shall not be able to deny. After dinner we will go through the manuscript together while Doctor Blandly sleeps."

" 'Tis burnt."

"No matter; I do believe I remember every word that you have wrote and read. I will recall the passages, and you shall write them."

"Lady Betty, you shall not waste your labours on a fruitless task. Give me your help and sympathy in achieving that which is within the power of an ordinary man, and we shall both succeed, you in holding me to my purpose, I in gaining the fair reward for my work."

"Why, that is well said, Gerard. Men do not live by writing plays alone. There are many honourable means of rising to eminence and fortune beside the stage. A poet's rank is not the noblest. Oh, you are wise and right. 'Tis only a woman who would attempt with pertinaceous obstinacy to obtain a position for which Nature unfitted her. And poets! what are they, Gerard? Lazy and indolent as a rule, careless in their persons, untidy in their habits. I wouldn't have you look less like a gentleman for all the adulation in the world. Then playwrights, again! Dear heart! what a life they lead! 'Tis said they drink and die prematurely, and the people they meet and speak to, and get to like behind the scenes! You would have lost your delicacy, you would have seen me but seldom, and then only to make me regret. I'm best pleased you have renounced the idea of writing plays for a profession; not that my opinion is altered in the least."

Gerard could only listen and love.

"You could have wrote a play as good as any of Mr. Garrick's, that's certain," she continued. "You can write for your own amusement and our pleasure; your theatre shall be the garden lawn, your audience good old Doctor Blandly and myself, with Mr. Baxter for a critic; his snore will be your only censure, unless you make the hero too bold. But you shall work for some higher end than the amusement of the idle. Couldn't you be an astronomer? There is something majestic in that study, and astronomers live to a great age. They seem to me almost as grand as patriarchs, and I never heard of one falling into bad habits."

"I fear it's a poor business in a lucrative sense. It would pay a man better to find five shillings than a new planet."

"Are you laughing at me?" Lady Betty asked, reproachfully.

"Laughing at you?" cried he, looking down with tumultuous emotion into her simple-wise, beautiful, grave face. "You dear! I could worship you for my God!"

He had taken her hand, and as he spoke he pressed it fiercely, and his ardent gaze seemed to scorch her very soul.

The blood left her face, she drew her hand from his and turned her eyes away with a frightened look. It struck her with the force of a sudden discovery that Gerard loved her, and loved her as a brother may not.

She walked to Doctor Blandly's gate without one word. Her silence contrasted oddly with her previous volubility. Gerard seemed equally embarrassed. His love was a secret no longer. Did he regret that a sudden accession of passion had overcome his habitual reserve? No.

The barrier was broken down, and the forces of love and passion took possession of his soul, sweeping reason and prudential considerations before them as they rushed from restraint.

"If she will let me hope to make her my wife," he said to himself, "what difficulty will be insurmountable? Position, money, whatsoever is necessary to her happiness, I will obtain, if she blesses me with that one encouragement."

And for this encouragement he prepared to ask her, when dinner should be finished, and Doctor Blandly taking his customary doze.

CHAPTER XV.

GERARD TURNS HIS FACE TO THE WALL.

"MY dear," said Doctor Blandly, after greeting Lady Betty, "when you have removed your bonnet and tippet, you will come and drink a glass of Madeira with me in the front room; our dinner will be a little later than usual to-day."

On Sunday, dinner was generally served at half-past one punctually, in order that Jerry and Kate might profit by the Reverend John Baxter's afternoon service, the present departure from that rule made no impression upon Lady Betty, whose thoughts were troubled by the recent discovery she had made of Gerard's feeling towards her. She ran upstairs to her room, and sat there for full five minutes in deep thought before commencing to make her toilette.

Meanwhile Doctor Blandly led Gerard into the front room, and insisted upon his drinking Madeira. Gerard was excited, and declared he felt no need of refreshment.

"Drink that, all the same," said the Doctor.

Gerard tossed off the glass with a laugh, and then said:

"I am afraid I have been the cause of your staying at home this morning, Sir."

"No, my boy; I have had visitors, and my time has been fully engaged—a remarkable thing for me, you will say. 'Tis true, a remarkable thing has occurred— a thing unexpected by me and by you."

"Something has happened to Barnabas," said Gerard, quickly.

"'Tis true. Will you have another glass of Madeira?"

"No; I can hear anything you have to tell me. Is he dead?"

"I will tell you all that has happened. Come with me into the garden. Lady Betty will be here presently, and you must know at once."

Gerard followed Doctor Blandly into the garden, impatient for a confirmation of his suspicions, and to tell the truth, of his hopes; for if Barnabas were dead, the Talbot estate would be his, and he should be able to offer Lady Betty something more than an empty hand. A young countryman in a worn livery was at the foot of the garden steps. Doctor Blandly whispered a word to him, and he, touching his hat, walked sharply down the garden, past the hedge and wicket, and into the kitchen-garden beyond.

"In the first place, Gerard," said the Doctor, touching the young man's arm, "I have seen the father of your half-brother Barnabas; he came yesterday, and offered to swear his paternity, and reveal the fraud put upon your father."

"That would put me in possession of my father's estate, and clear his name from disgrace."

"So I thought, and I bade the man come to-morrow to know if you would buy his services. But listen, he had no sooner gone than I learnt a still more important fact. You saw the young fellow to whom I just now spoke?"

"The country servant."

"He is a foolish and dense, but in the main, honest lad. He has served Barnabas —partly compelled by fear, partly cheated by a mistaken idea of gratitude. He detailed the circumstance of Toms disappearance. Tom was thrown from his horse, and while he lay stunned upon the ground, Barnabas shot him. At the same moment, Tom's horse, in struggling to rise, kicked Barnabas, breaking his leg. Unable to re-mount, and fancying he heard the sound of approaching voices, he called for assistance to the lad—Toby Slink, whom he had placed in ambush near at hand. Slink carried him into an adjacent corn-field, and in obeyance to his threats and command, returned to the towpath to throw Tom's body into the river.

"As he laid his hand on Tom's arm, your brother opened his eyes. The fall had stunned him; the bullet had passed through the fleshy part of his arm. When the lad recovered from his fright, he went down on his knees, and prayed to Tom to forgive him, acknowledging the part he had been sent to play. Tom was weak from the loss of blood, still bewildered by the blow, and knew that he was at the lad's mercy. He had no reason to suspect the identity of Barnabas, and no suspicion of what would result from his disappearance, so he promised the lad to hide for a fair month, giving him a chance of escaping from his master, and avoiding the punishment Barnabas had vowed to inflict if his orders were not carried out successfully. For Tom had left London with the intention of staying aloof from Lady Betty, until his unreasonable jealousy was cured, and here was a means which he thought——"

"How do you know what Tom thought?" Gerard asked, turning deadly pale.

"Because he has told me. He is at the bottom of the garden at this moment, as hale and hearty, thank God, as ever he was."

Gerard dropped his chin upon his breast, and murmured—

"I also *should* thank God."

"And you will, dear lad, when this momentary pang of loss has passed," said the Doctor tenderly. "For he who did most sacrifice, has said that 'tis more blessed to give than to receive."

With an effort Gerard seemed to free himself from regretful reflection, as raising his head quickly, he looked down the garden towards that part where his brother waited.

"Go to him, Gerard," said the Doctor; "I hear Betty's voice."

They separated after a silent grasp of hands, Doctor Blandly going into the house, Gerard through the wicket, and down the fresh-scented vegetable-garden. The brothers met and embraced, after the fashion of that time, but in silence, and then they sat down side by side on the bench where Doctor Blandly was wont to sit and admire his healthy cabbages and bright scarlet beans.

"Where is my Betty, Gerard?" Tom asked, in a low, eager voice.

"In the house still, with Doctor Blandly."

"I hunger to see her sweet face again; the Doctor tells me that she is looking thiner and paler than she did."

"She has suffered, Tom, and for love of you."

"Poor soul! poor child! Dear sweetheart! She shall smile from this day; she shall laugh and dance and sing, and not a grave thought shall come to her of my making. You will see the bright life stream into her face like colour to the opening bud, Gerard; you shall see her more happy than the bird upon the bough there; so that it will do your heart good to look upon her."

"Yes, yes," Gerard answered.

"The Doctor has told me of her courage, her independence, her fidelity and trust, outdoing my imagination, and shaming my hopes as all too mean and contracted. Walk with me, Gerard, I cannot sit still. Great God, how abundant are thy blessings!"

Gerard rose and walked by his side, glad of any change that would help him to conceal his feelings.

"'Tis all incredible!" continued Tom. "To think that when I saw you last, sitting beside Lady Betty in your chariot the morning of our duel, I was a hopeless fallen wretch, standing hid amongst the shrubs, putting an ill-construction upon her smiles and gaiety."

"Poor soul—she was half-mad for joy that you had escaped."

"I know it. I have felt sure that it was so in my reasonable moments, but then I was mad with jealousy and shame, and could be just to no one. I felt myself then alone in the world, despised, laughed at, loveless, and now I find that I am loved as never man was loved before, I think. My Betty, my wife!"

"She has ever thought of you as her husband."

"Blandly has told me so, and of her love for you because you were my brother. Truth—love has driven that joy from my remembrance. 'Tis not alone I find a wife, but a brother too. Give me your hand, brother—both. You also have done brave things. I am told you have writ a play."

"A worthless play as it proves—Mr. Kemble has damned it."

"Then damn Mr. Kemble in return. Pshaw! you shall do better than write plays for a grudged remuneration; you shall see 'em for your pleasure, Gerard;

one half of all I have is yours, all if you will, so that I have my Betty."

"Then you would be the richer, Tom."

"Aye, that I should, a hundredfold. We will live together, hunt together, fetch long walks, and live as brothers should. We will share a happiness in common, and when we find a suitable wife for you— some sweet, good girl ——"

He broke off suddenly, for his ear caught above the sound of his own voice a faint cry:

"Tom—my spouse!"

Lady Betty had run across the lawn, had reached the wicket by the hedge, and then hearing his well-remembered voice, her strength failed her, and she held by the gate, her knees trembling beneath her, crying and sobbing so that for awhile she could make no articulate sound.

At her cry he came, and seeing him she tottered forward with a little scream, and would have fallen but that he caught her up in his arms and held her to his heart. And then she pressed her lips to his, and swooned away with the ecstacy of her joy.

Gerard turned his face to the wall.

CHAPTER XVI.

THE OMEN.

THE company did spare justice to the excellent dinner prepared by old Kate. The lovers were impatient of the moments that kept their hands and eyes asunder; Doctor Blandly was excited; and every morsel that he forced himself to take seemed to choke Gerard. For Lady Betty's peace he was bound to be there, though for his own he would fain have been alone in a desert.

After dinner, Doctor Blandly mercifully

despatched him with a note to Mr. Baxter, and instructions to bring the parson back to share in the general happiness, while he, with many apologies for the infirmity of his old age, ensconsed himself in his elbow-chair, and did his utmost to sleep as usual. He may have failed, but what took place between the lovers was concealed from his sight by the yellow silk handkerchief.

During the afternoon Jerry brought up the best that his master's cellar contained, and under the influence of the wine the Reverend John Baxter and Doctor Blandly became excessively merry.

Lady Betty's spirits mounted also, but her gaiety was hysterical, and towards evening, in the midst of a peal of laughter, she caught sight of Gerard's face, and as suddenly burst into a flood of tears.

Doctor Blandly came to her side, and when he had calmed her he insisted upon her going to bed. She did not refuse to use the spare chamber, and soon after Mr. Baxter returned to the Vicarage with an explanation for his wife.

The brothers and Doctor Blandly sat together and talked.

"What has become of my half-brother, Barnabas?" Gerard asked.

"Ah, I have that part of my history to tell you," replied Tom. "When I returned to the Hall, the first thing I did was to frighten old Blake nearly out of his wits. He is an egotist, and having come to the conclusion that I had been murdered by Barnabas, I believe his dignity was hurt by seeing me alive."

"He is a conceited old fool," said the Doctor.

"But a faithful servant, so we will forgive him his faults. When I had reconciled him to the fact of entertaining a wrong conviction, he told me of the life Barnabas has led as the master of Talbot Hall. A most wretched, miserable existence it must have been."

"Vice and happiness are as far asunder as love and hate," said Doctor Blandly, sententiously.

"Deserted by everyone, the unhappy man had left the Hall, Blake knew not why, possibly to find relief from solitude in the nearest inn. When we went up to the house we could find no one, but as I wished to see him I sat down to wait for his return. I heard from the steward all that had happened. The light faded and we lit candles. When Blake had nothing more to tell, he fell asleep. The rain fell pitilessly, and as I sat there listening to the perpetual dripping, I fancied what the condition of a guilty wretch would be, deserted and alone in that old hall, and I commiserated the man who had attempted my life."

"A mistake, Tom, a mistake," said the Doctor; "commiserate the unfortunate, if you will, but whip all rogues, I say."

"You may say that, Doctor; but your practice would be most merciful. For what are rogues but unfortunate? Have you not said that vice and happiness are wide asunder?"

"Go on with your facts, Tom. You can philosophise better when you are older."

"When the monotony was becoming insupportable, I heard a sound outside. I roused Blake. We listened, and soon after a faint whistle reached our ears. I went to the window, and looking out caught sight of a lantern by the terrace steps. Blake took a candle, and we went into the entrance-hall. He was fearful, and standing well behind the door, pulled it open and raised the light that I might see who was without. There was a shock upon the stone pavement like the fall of a tile from the roof, and taking the candle from Blake I found, stretched at full length, the man who had attempted my life—Barnabas, to appearance dead. We got him into the hall, and after awhile, when he showed signs of returning consciousness, I withdrew, leaving him to Blake's rough mercy. What means he took to assure him that he had nothing to fear from me I can't tell."

"If Blake's the man I take him for he promised him nothing short of hanging, I'll be bound," said Doctor Blandly.

"That is not unlikely, for as soon as Barnabas had recovered his strength he knocked the old man down, and fled from the Hall, whither it is impossible to say. The outbuildings were all closed, the rain fell in a torrent the whole night, it was pitch dark, and the unhappy wretch was lame. He did not return to the Hall.

In the morning Blake wished to have the woods beat, and to hunt him out like a fox, but as this might have driven him to some deplorable act of desperation, I forbade any search to be made beyond the outbuildings and parksweep. I waited about the Hall until late in the afternoon, hoping he would return, for in the course of the day I learnt from the innkeeper near that he had no money, and I expected that hunger would force him to come back to the Hall. However, I had seen no sign of him when I quitted Sevenoaks yesterday evening. I left orders that food should be put in the hall, and the doors left open, and that he should be unmolested."

"Thank you, Tom, for your forbearance," said Gerard; "I have wished him dead again and again, but he is my mother's son, and I would not have him die a shameful death."

"God forbid!" said Doctor Blandly. "'Tis a barbarous and a mischievous thing to publicly kill a man in infamy. The proper end of punishment is, to correct and deter, and for a rogue like Barnabas, death is no punishment at all. The scaffold makes heroes of contemptible villains. Punish rascals, I say again, despite Master Tom's merciful outcry, but punish them in a manner that shall teach them the policy of living decently."

"You shall tell us, Doctor, how we are to punish him, for I confess 'tis a question that perplexes me," said Tom.

The Doctor knitted his brows, pursed up his lips, and took a deliberate pinch of snuff before replying; then he said:

"I would just pay his passage to America or another of our colonies, and give the captain a round sum to be handed to him for his necessities when he is set ashore."

"And the whipping you suggested?" Tom asked, slyly.

"You can promise him that if ever he shows his face in England again. I take it that what with fright, starvation, a broken leg, and exposure to the rain of Friday night, he has had as much corporal punishment as his constitution can support; 'tis his conscience that must chastise him henceforth."

As neither of the brothers could suggest any improvement upon Doctor Blandly's proposed dealing with Barnabas, it was determined between them that the following day they should post to Sevenoaks, find Barnabas, and make terms with him for quitting the country.

When Lady Betty woke, the morning was yet grey. She slipped from her white nest, and running across to the window drew back a corner of the blind and looked down into the garden, Tom was there; it was not too early for a lover to be up. Making a frame with the blind, she showed him her smiling face, closed her red lips and parted them; he seemed to understand the pantomime, and recklessly tearing a rose which Doctor Blandly would have grudgingly nipped with careful scissors, he threw it up upon her window-sill in response. In an incredibly short space of time she dressed, and with his flower in her bosom ran down, and gave up her still sweeter, tenderer face to his lips.

He put his arm about her and she

clasped his hand, and in that position they walked round the garden dozens of times, looking at the flowers but not thinking of them; feeling the utmost happiness but saying very little, perhaps because all words seemed too prosaic to express the poetry of their love.

" We are not talking much," she said after awhile, with a little laugh.

" I do love you so, darling, that I cannot think of indifferent matters readily. I love you, that is all my tongue will say."

" 'Tis enough, dear," she answered.

She was right, perhaps; but after awhile he felt it necessary to say something else.

" You have more colour in your sweet cheeks this morning," said he, " did you sleep well ?"

" Too well. I said to myself when I closed my eyes—' I will dream of Tom, or I will not sleep at all;' but my eyes closed, and I don't remember dreaming anything pretty—only a lot of confused rubbish that was not worth dreaming about at all. Now what *did* I dream?— Oh!" she stopped suddenly, with a frightened look.

"Something terrible?"

"I dreamt that I lost a tooth."

Tom burst into a hearty laugh, but Lady Betty looked grave.

"You little goose," he cried, "are you vexed because you did not dream of Cupids and roses?"

"No, but do you know what that signifies?"

"Not in the least, unless it be that dreams going by contraries, you will shortly cut your wisdom tooth, sweet."

"Don't laugh, Tom; I believe in dreams."

"So do I, when they are pleasantly

realised. And what is the significance of yours?"

"I shall lose a friend."

"Why that may be true enough, for you will lose me for a whole day."

"Where are you going, dear?" she asked with anxiety.

Tom told briefly the arrangement he had made with Gerard to seek Barnabas.

"You are going to find the man who tried to take your life!" she exclaimed. "Oh, if you love me, dear, don't leave me."

She was so earnest that Tom became grave. Women and men with greater wisdom than Lady Betty believed at that time in signs and omens, and however absurd they may have appeared to Tom, he saw nothing ridiculous in the fear of his sweetheart for his safety.

"Dear love," said he, "we are nowhere safe from accident. And if there be truth in omens, 'tis well to take their lightest interpretation. What will the loss be then but our separation for a day?"

"Are you obliged to go, dear?" Lady Betty asked, the subject not being one for argument.

"Be sure 'tis necessity that takes me away from you, love."

"There is danger—will you not stay with me if I ask you?"

"Yes. I will do anything you bid me do; but I do not think Lady Betty will ask her husband to forgo a duty for the sake of safety."

"Kiss me, love, and forgive me for forgetting your honour. Do what *you* will, brave darling, and heed me not. I am nothing but a little woman—with a woman's love and fear. . . . There! now I will not say another word to hinder your purpose."

CHAPTER XVII.

A STURDY ROGUE.

"JERRY," said Doctor Blandly, when the old servant brought him his customary tankard at breakfast, "you will see that the two saddle horses are ready at the "Bell" by half past ten."

"I'll go round if you please, Sir, and give the hostler a good talking to at once."

"Do; then take this letter to Mr. Baxter; and afterwards find the constable, and tell him to be here about ten o'clock."

Jerry departed at once to execute these commissions, and Doctor Blandly explained the little comedy that would probably be played before Tom and Gerard left.

As ten o'clock struck, Barney O'Crewe rang the bell, and thoughtfully stroking his scrubby chin, went over for the last time those delicate points which would come under discussion in the forthcoming interview with Doctor Blandly.

"The top o' the mornun to you, squoire," he said as Jerry opened the gate and admitted him. "Is the Docthor widin, if ye plase?"

"I shouldn't let you in if he wasn't," answered Jerry, fastening the gate.

"I'm deloighted to foind ye as agraable and complaisint as usual; an' if I can putt a word in for ye wid the master, I will, be sure, squoire."

Jerry made no reply, but led the way into the house, and opening the door of the breakfast-room, introduced the pedlar.

The breakfast things were still upon the table. Doctor Blandly sat at the head, with Tom on one side of him and the Reverend John Baxter on the other. Lady Betty seated beside Tom, rested her right hand lightly upon the table, her left, lost to sight, was locked in his; opposite to her, and with his back towards the door, sat Gerard.

"Me sarvice to ye, me lady, and to you, Docthor Blandly, and to your riverince, and likwoise to you, gentlemen," said the pedlar, with a bow to each. "It seems that the owld man has played an onsamely trick upon me, Docthor, to bring me here, where ye sit surrounded by the quality on both sides of ye."

"No; he obeyed my orders. We are

all friends of Mr. Talbot." Doctor Blandly replied, with a motion of his hand towards Tom.

"Mr. Gerard, Sor, I salutes ye wid all the respect in the world." The pedlar bowed again to Tom. "Shure I knowed ye the vary moment I clapped eyes on ye, for yer the vary image of your swate mother —the saints in heaven bless her sowl."

"I have given Mr. Talbot your narrative of Saturday, but in case I have omitted any particular, it will be well for you to repeat what you told me for our general satisfaction," said Doctor Blandly.

"And I should be proud to do that same, Docthor; but ye must know I've a tremenjous objaction to spaking in public. I can contrive to spake in private; but I'm so modest and bashful that I could niver get out a word before such a collection of the quality."

"I don't ask you to say anything which

will affect your negociation with Mr. Gerard; all that I desire is that you will repeat the statement you made relative to the attack upon Mr. Thomas Talbot—which I understood you to say you had sworn before a magistrate."

"Sure it's thrue, every word of it, and I've sworn it upon the Horly Bible before the magistrate, as ye say, though for the loife of me I don't remember the name of um at this minute."

"That is what I wish you to state now. Afterwards, if Mr. Talbot pleases, you can privately make terms for any further revelations that are necessary."

"Doctor Blandly expresses my wish," said Tom. "Before I enter into any negociation with you I must have particulars of the murder committed by Slink."

"Y'are roight, dear Mr. Gerard, y'are quite roight to take your precautions, for y'are not supposed to know but what I'm the greatest scoundrel goun. And sure if 'tis only to tell you all about the murtherin varmint, Slink, I can overcome my nat'ral hesitation." The pedlar cleared his throat, and looking at the good things upon the table with a longing eye, said: " Docther, will ye give me a taste o' wather to give me courage, and moisten my lips?"

" You may take some water, there is a glass and the bottle."

With a wry face O'Crewe poured out about a spoonful of water in the glass, which he raised to his lips and set down again with the remark, that it was a " moighty onpleasant flavour" the water had in these parts; and then with all the effrontery of a Newgate pleader, he repeated in substance the story he had told to Doctor Blandly, but with many rhetorical flourishes and eloquent additions, for the old man was vain of his ability, and only too proud to make a display before a cultivated audience. He addressed himself chiefly to Tom, under the impression that he was Gerard, but pathetic passages he delivered looking at Lady Betty, as when he described the " swate smoile that dwelt on the young murthered gintleman's face as he looked up to the blessed stars above 'um," and when, in conclusion, he called upon the saints in Heaven to witness that he had no object but to prove the holy truth, he directed his glance to the Reverend John Baxter.

" Perhaps we can prove the truth without troubling the saints," said Doctor Blandly, drily, as he touched the bell.

O'Crewe opened his eyes in astonishment. Jerry entered.

" Tell the constable to bring the young man here," said Doctor Blandly.

The constable presently appeared leading Slink by the arm.

"Do you know who that is?" asked Doctor Blandly.

"Do I know who it is? I should think I did! Sorra a one better. 'Tis the murtherin varmint, Slink himself, wid just the same bloodthirsty expression in the face of 'um he had when I see 'um a dragging that swate blessed Misther Tom into the cowld, cowld river!"

Slink grinned from ear to ear.

"Don't laugh, ye murtherin' villain, ye'll not escape the vingeance of the law. I know ye at once, though I nivir saw yer face but twoice in my loife."

"You have a good memory for features," said Doctor Blandly; "do you remember the face of Mr. Thomas Talbot?"

"Nothun better; I shall never forget the expression of 'um to my dyun day. He was not like you, Mr. Gerard, for ye've got the faitures of your mother, and Mr. Tom tuk afther the owld admiral."

At this assertion Slink was attacked with such a fit of laughter that he had to bend his body at a right angle with his legs, and stamp his feet before he could fetch breath. In a less demonstrative fashion the rest of the company seemed also amused.

"Sor!" exclaimed O'Crewe, addressing Doctor Blandly, and drawing himself up with an air of offended dignity, "wad ye be koind enough to explain the manin' o' that dirty blackgyard's behavior?"

"The explanation is this," said Tom, "my name is Thomas Talbot."

"Mr. Thomas! and not dead at all? Thank the powers!" said O'Crewe, with ready wit. "I'm rejoiced to see you lookun so well, Sor, an' it plases me moightily to foind that I've been makun a mistake all the while."

"But it doesn't please me," cried the Doctor; "and if you have sworn a lie you shall be punished for your perjury."

"Sure, and that was a mistake too, Docthor dear. D'ye think I'd swear the life away of a charmun young innocint country lad? divil a bit! I never swored, nothun at all, at all." As he spoke the pedlar edged away from the constable towards the door.

"Wait," said the Reverend John Baxter; "there's one thing that there is no mistake about. You have tried to impose on us with a false and scandalous assertion."

"Sure your riverence that was the greatest mistake of all."

"And one that you shall have the opportunity of repenting. Constable, you will take this man and lock up his feet in the stocks until sundown. Give him as much water as he can drink, and no more bread than he can pay for—off with him for a sturdy rogue."

CHAPTER XVIII.

FAREWELL.

CHANGING horses twice upon the road, Tom and Gerard reached Talbot Hall about five o'clock in the afternoon. Old Blake came to the gate.

"He's about, Sir—he's about," he said, in a low voice. "He was seen yesterday, and I catched sight of him again this morning. Shall I fetch my gun and come up to the house with you?"

Tom laughed. "Do you think we need protection against a poor lame devil such as he? Open the gate, and come up to us in half-an-hour, and not before."

Blake shook his head, and reluctantly opened the gate for the two gentlemen to pass.

"Go on, Gerard; I will overtake you in a couple of minutes. It has just struck me that Slink's sweetheart is dying to know his fate," Tom said, pulling up when they were half-dozen yards from the lodge. He turned his horse and walked back, while Gerard, waiting for him, cast his eyes over the wide spread of lawn, and along the terrace before the house. Not a living thing was to be seen.

Half way up the long drive there was on either side a clump of evergreens; they were the only places of concealment between the lodge and the house. As he was looking at them, a rabbit hopped out from the clump on the right hand side into the gravelled path, and standing on his hind legs with his ears cocked, regarded him for a moment, then leisurely hopped over towards the left hand clump. Just as it reached the turf, it stopped suddenly, and then with a sharp turn from the evergreens, it flew off towards the woods as fast as it could lay its heels to the ground. Why, if it were frightened, did it not seek shelter in the thickly-planted covert? Gerard asking himself the question, shifted his horse from the right to the left hand side of the path, as Tom with a nod to the girl he had been making happy with a few kind words, trotted away from the lodge, and came to his brother's side.

"What do you think of the Hall, Gerard?"

"'Tis a fine building."

"One wing is closed altogether; the other needs repair. A few rooms in the centre are the only really habitable ones at present. But we will alter all that. We will go over the whole place and arrange together what changes will be necessary to make it a pleasant home. What are you looking at, Gerard?"

"This is a noble lawn, Tom."

"Oh, 'tis the lawn you are looking at. I thought you had caught sight of game in the covert. There are deer in the park, and when they come upon the lawn, they add to the prettiness of the picture; but a sweet wife on the terrace, and children stretching their pretty arms out to welcome us, are wanting to make it perfect——"

"May nothing be wanting to complete your happiness."

"Nor yours, Gerard. I see nothing of that unhappy man, do you?"

"Nothing," said Gerard.

They had passed the clumps, Gerard riding between that on the left and Tom, and were now close to the house. They dismounted, and having hitched their reins upon the iron scroll-work at the foot of the terrace steps, they entered the house by the open door.

Tom threw open the door of the dining-room. It was empty; upon the table were scraps of broken food, an overturned pitcher and a dirty glass half full of stale ale. They examined room after room, and finding no one, went out beyond the shrubberies into the stables; they also were deserted. Here they were joined by Blake.

" Where are the horses ?" asked Tom.

"I've had 'em removed, Sir," replied the steward. " For you see, Sir, this Mr. —Mr. Crewe, I think he's called, lost his'n, and I thought he might take a fancy to breaking a lock, and taking one of yourn, Sir. Lord, Sir, 'taint no good looking about for him in there. He's as scary as a hunted fox. When I see him this morning he was eating food a-standing in the hall-doorway, to make sure he shouldn't be trapped—he's as wild as a Bedlamite. This was the stall where he kep' his horse, and that his saddle."

"Come into the house, Gerard. Blake, send something to eat and drink up to my room. What can you give us?"

Discussing the question of refreshment, Tom and the steward walked out of the stable. Gerard following them, stepped aside quickly to the hanging saddle and put his hand into the holsters: they were empty.

The room chosen by Tom for his use was above the entrance, and looked down upon the terrace. They sat near the window and ate, and when the meal was finished they walked round the Hall and along the terrace until the light faded, then they returned to the chamber, having seen nothing of Barnabas. Rain was beginning to fall again.

"Gerard, we must put an end to that poor wretch's sufferings to-morrow. It is terrible to think of him wandering about half starved in this atrocious weather, without shelter or a single comfort in the world. If he is wild with fear, as Blake makes out he is, we are not likely to get within speaking distance of him unless we take measures for catching him. That will not be a difficult task with the servants to help us, as he is lame; but one has a natural repugnance to hunting a human creature as one would a beast."

"True; yet, as you say, he must not be suffered to exist in his present manner, and if we cannot find a better method before the morning, that must be adopted."

"I am anxious on your account, as well as his. 'Tis preying on your mind, Gerard, to an extreme. I understand how you must feel upon the subject, but I confess your depression astonishes me. You have known him long for a scoundrel, and thought him your brother. 'Tis some satisfaction to know that his father was not yours."

"I feel that, Tom; and admit that the balance of fortune has lately turned in my favour."

"Then why shouldn't you be of better cheer? The future is not unpleasant to you; we shall share everything, and you will find me eager to catch your wishes and fall in with them."

"I know, I know," Gerard said, pressing the hand his brother held out to him.

"You have no secret grief, hey, brother? I never knew anyone so utterly dejected, except myself, when I fancied that my mistress despised me. You have not lost a sweetheart, have you?"

"A sweetheart," Gerard said, with a

dry laugh. "Did you ever hear of me loving a woman, do you think a woman could love me, an ex-gamester, brother to a murdering villain, a man who succeeds at fleecing fools at cards and fails in the first honest work to which he set his hand? The most that an angel can do is to pity me."

"'Tis but the thought of to-day, Gerard. A year—six months—aye, less than that, of companionship with pleasant folks, will change your bitter reflections upon the past to sweet hopes of a future. I shall take my wife to Italy while the alterations are being made here, and you shall come with us, and if my sweet Betty's lively happiness does not drive away your care, I will suffer you to build a cell and live in it like a hermit."

Gerard turned away in silence.

"Well, well, think what you will," said Tom, "time shall show. Fill your glass, and when the bottle is empty we will turn into bed. Will you share my room, or take the next?"

"I'll take the next, for the sake of having my own sweet company to myself."

"As you will, Gerard."

"I'll say good-night now. Is the library door unlocked?"

"Yes."

"I shall read for an hour. Good-night, Tom."

"God bless you, Gerard."

CHAPTER XIX.

IN THE LIBRARY.

THE library, like all the principal rooms in Talbot Hall, looked out upon the terrace. The shutters were unclosed, and the heavy curtains looped up. The light of the candle lit by Gerard could be seen from the lawn.

Gerard sat with his legs crossed and his hands clasped over his knee for full half-an-hour in thought; then he rose, took the first book that his hand touched, and opening it in the middle, read. He raised his head and listened, catching a faint sound from the outside; but the swinging of a lantern and a heavy regular tread growing distinct, he dropped his eyes again. The outer door was opened, and someone tapped at the library door.

"Come in," he said.

Blake entered, his collar up, a stream of water falling from his hat as he removed it.

"Beg your pardon, Sir, is Mr. Thomas here?" he asked.

"No; he is in the room upstairs."

"No light in the window, Sir."

"Then he is asleep, or, at least, in bed."

"Any orders for the morning, Sir?"

"Tell one of the stable lads to have a horse ready as soon as it is light."

"Right, Sir. The lad shall sleep in the stable, and when you want the horse

—if you'll just give him a call—his name's Jacob, Sir."

"Very well. Good-night."

"Beg your pardon, Sir, shall I show you how to fasten the front door."

"No, I understand that."

"That's everything, Sir. I only mentioned it because I see something like a figure round the shrubbery in the dusk, and——"

Gerard nodded, and returning to his book, closed further discussion.

The retreating step of the old steward, and subsequently the heavy step of a stable-help, were the only sounds that broke the silence for a couple of hours; during that time Gerard read page after page of the book on his knee listlessly. He read because he could not sleep and did not want to think.

The wind had risen, and blew the rain in gusty violence against the windows, now in a sharp, momentary dash, and again in a long, pattering volley; but the casements were well secured, and the lights burnt steadily by Gerard's side. After a long pelting of heavy drops against the glass, the wind turned, and there was a lull in the stormy brunt. In this momentary silence, a grating sound fell upon Gerard's ear, and simultaneously the flame of the candles swept down the wax and leapt up, confusing the printed lines under his eye. Had the wind blown open the front door? It was hardly possible, the steward had closed it carefully, and tried it afterwards with his knee.

Yet clearly the wind had entered by some opening, Gerard felt the damp chill of it upon his face. He raised his eyes from the page to the library door. He could not see it distinctly for the light that fell between. He moved the candelabra further back, then replaced his hand upon the book, keeping his eyes upon the door latch, and moving not a muscle. Presently he saw the latch rise and slowly descend as the door moved beyond the catch. Little by little the door moved forward upon its hinges, and the opening gradually yawned. Suddenly it flew back, and in the uncertain light Gerard distinguished Barnabas bringing up a pistol to the level of his head.

Gerard sat as motionless as a statue. He might have been dead already, but for the reflected light in his eyes, and that he spoke:

" Barnabas," he said.

Barnabas lowered his pistol, and looking quickly round the room, his finger still upon the trigger, asked hoarsely:

" Where is he ?"

" Asleep."

" You spoke just in time. Curse the

light, I cannot see. Is he hiding here? Mark me, 'twill be your fault if I am a fratricide, for by God I'll shoot you if he lays a finger upon me in treachery!"

He spoke, looking round the room wildly, and evidently as a warning to Tom if he were in concealment.

"He is not here. If you don't want to wake him, shut the door and speak lower."

"Shut the door! A likely thing, I'm not trapped yet. Speak low! What do I want to say to you? Nothing. What I have to say to him this will tell!" He made a movement with the heavy pistol.

"What good will it do you to shoot him? Are you mad?"

"Nearly. I have been quite. And it was he drove me out of my senses coming before me and standing there in

the doorway when I thought he was dead.
A fine joke for him, but one that will cost
him dear. Let him come, I don't fear
him now. The rain and pain, and hunger
and thirst have cured me. I've another
friend in my pocket, and standing here,
in this corner, I fear none of you—my
father, Slink, him, you, and all that are
plotting to do for me."

He put himself in the corner by the
door, and lugged out the second pistol
from his pocket, looking now in the dark
behind him, now towards Gerard and the
room.

Gerard, becoming more used to the
dim light, could mark the appearance of
his half-brother. His dress was torn
with briars. A great rent in his sleeve
exposed his bare forearm and elbow; the
rain beating upon his face showed it a
ghastly white where it was not covered
with a thick, scrubby beard; he had lost

his hat, and his hair hung matted about his head, dripping with rain.

"If you are not mad, you are a fool," said Gerard. "If we sought to give you up to the law should we come unarmed to do the work of constable? Tom Talbot has come here to offer you money and an escape from the country."

"I should be mad or a fool indeed to believe that! Do you think I or anyone else would give money and help to a man who had done his utmost to murder me? And that's what you would have me believe: well then my answer is, you are a liar."

"Think of what I have said, and come again to me in an hour. By that time you will see the folly of supposing that we are here with treacherous intentions."

"Oh, I know your sneaking gentlemanly ways. You who can rob, and cheat, swindle and thieve a rich living with no tools but a pack of cards and a dice box, have a quicker and surer means of cheating a low rogue like me than I can readily guess at. I know why the doors have been left open, and food put upon the table—to tempt me and trap me like a rat into a cage. I said to myself— these things are not set here for nothing, in a day or two my lord Tom with a sneaking hound or two at his heels will come to play out the farce to a conclusion. I've been waiting for him, and I would have shot him dead this afternoon, for his white coat was a sure mark, but that you, plague you, got between him and me."

"And if you had shot him—what then?"

"What then—the gallows, a brave face, the cheers of the mob, and a sudden death. Isn't that a better end than rotting away year by year in a gaol."

"No one wishes to serve you so."

"You liar!" Barnabas said, grating his teeth. "I've a mind to put a bullet in your pretty body, you sneaking, gentlemanly thief." He trembled with envious hate, and half raised his pistol.

"Go out, and reflect on what I have said; I shall sit here until the morning and will listen to any terms you like to make. But I warn you that you will have no longer than this night to consider. To-morrow morning we shall name our terms and oblige you to accept them."

"Not while I can lift a pistol. I swear I will hang for the man who has made my life hell to me, and for once I will keep my oath."

At this moment there was a movement above, and Barnabas looked into the darkness with palpable fear. He was like a beast at bay, for whom a sound has more terror than a blow. He was a coward even in his desperation.

Tom's voice above called, "Gerard!"

In a moment Barnabas dashed from his corner, and fled out into the darkness. Gerard heard him stumbling down the terrace steps.

"Gerard," Tom called, again.

Gerard made no reply. Tom, too drowsy to make inquiries into the noise that had disturbed him, turned upon his side to sleep and dream. Gerard sat and watched.

And the night wore slowly on.

CHAPTER XX.

"GREATER LOVE HATH NO MAN THAN THIS, THAT A MAN LAY DOWN HIS LIFE FOR HIS FRIENDS."

GERARD paced up and down the library. He could fix his attention upon the book no longer. From time to time he walked to the window and looked out into the obscurity; once he went out to the door in the entrance-hall, peering to the right and left along the terrace. He could see nothing. He had but slight hope of Barnabas returning, and when at length the outline of the distant woods became vaguely visible, he felt convinced that the resolution Barnabas had made was unalterable. He would surely take Tom's life.

He stood for a few minutes with his hand resting on the table, looking round the room, and he pictured the future. The room glowing with the light of burning logs in the wide chimney ; his brother Tom seated there with Lady Betty, his sweet wife, beside him; Doctor Blandly an honoured guest sharing their happiness and content, and little children playing at their mother's feet. There was no vacant chair placed for an expected friend in the picture. With a sigh he turned away and walked to the end of the room, where in the evening they had thrown down their hats and coats.

He took up Tom's light drab riding-coat and drew it on. It was large for him—so much the better for his purpose.

When he turned up the collar and buttoned it over it covered the lower half of his face. Then he put on his hat, drawing it down over his eyes. Thus dressed, even in the light he might have been mistaken for his brother Tom.

He paused in walking towards the door, asking himself if he should write a word to leave behind him—a message to her—to him—a testimony of the love in his heart? No, 'twould but add to their sorrow if they knew him for something better than an unfortunate man. The family Bible was in his hand; he might have left it open upon the table with the page turned down at this line: "Greater love has no man than this, that a man lay down his life for his friends." Should he do so to tell how much he loved? No, 'twould be less painful to attribute his end to unfortunate carelessness than heroic design.

He went out of the Hall leaving no message; breathing only a prayer for the happiness of those who should live there after he was gone.

The wind had abated and the rain ceased to fall heavily; but over the dark grey sky black clouds hurried quickly, huge and formless. The terrace was clear, and the long drive could be seen for some yards before it was lost in the vapoury gloom.

Gerard walked round slowly by the shrubbery seeing no one, and coming to the stable he called "Jacob."

The stable lad answered readily, and having struck a light with the flint, quickly put a saddle on Tom's horse. Suddenly in passing Gerard he stopped:

"I ax your pardon, Sir," said he, "but I've gone and saddled the wrong mare; I thought you was Master Thomas by the coat."

"No matter, the mare will do. Lead her out."

The mare was led out, and Gerard sprang into the saddle.

"You can put the light out and go to sleep again, Jacob. Take this."

"Thankye, Sir, thankye kindly," said the lad, spitting on the crown Gerard had put in his hand. For him the day was beginning well.

Gerard walked his horse past the shrubbery and into the drive. It was growing light rapidly. After walking down the broad path a hundred yards, Gerard could discern the outlines of the two evergreen clumps standing by the path.

"All that heaven gives to happy mortals be theirs—my brother and his wife," he said to himself. "He will grow stout and florid, Tom; with a love for creature comforts and healthy sports. Kind to his fellows, loving his children better than his life, and loving his wife dearer than all. An honest, healthy, English country gentleman. And she will reign like a queen in his house, beautiful and fair, making all love her by her simple fidelity and gentleness. God bless them! I have no other wish."

Paug-ker!

With the report came a flash of light from amidst the evergreens, and a bullet sped straight to the heart of Gerard. His last wish was uttered; his sorrows done; his end come.

The mare started forward, jerking the dead body from the saddle.

"There shall be no mistake this time," muttered Barnabas, throwing aside the used pistol and drawing another from his pocket as he scrambled through the evergreens.

With his arms spread out like a cross, Gerard lay, with his face upwards to the light. As Barnabas recognised his half-brother, his soul, callous as it was, shrunk within him.

His first idea was of the consequences. That the mob would not applaud as he looked down on the thousand faces from the scaffold—that they would drag him from the tumbril, and tear him limb from limb, was the thought that presented itself to his mind. Not a regret, nor the faintest tinge of remorse, touched him; only fear. And already he heard voices and approaching feet.

He looked round like a hunted brute, closed his eyes, and put the muzzle of his pistol slowly to his mouth; then, with his thumb, he pressed the trigger.

* * * *

THE END.

www.ingramcontent.com/pod-product-compliance
Lightning Source LLC
Chambersburg PA
CBHW030820230426
43667CB00008B/1300